LAUGH UNTIL YOUR RIBS HURT
INTERNET COMPILATION OF JOKES
2000-2010

BY ASTRA PACOLD

Aventine Press

Published by Aventine Press
750 State St. #319
San Diego CA, 92101
www.aventinepress.com

ISBN: 1-59330-692-X

Library of Congress Control Number: 2010916720
Library of Congress Cataloging-in-Publication Data
Laugh Until Yiur Ribs Hurt

Printed in the United States of America

TABLE OF CONTENTS

CHAPTER 0

FOREWORD

The last 10 years has given rise to all my friends who communicate on the Internet to send jokes. We e-mail jokes back and forth for many reasons. We like to laugh. It makes others laugh. We communicate in busy days to release stress or strain of our serious world at work. We share a common bond to tickle that funny bone or to get ribbed. I have saved all the jokes for a last 10 years that were e-mailed to me. I wanted to write this book even for those who do not have a computer to laugh and to enjoy humor. There is something cathartic about reading jokes. The value of laughter is not only healthy but opens the mind to work and to play in a positive manner.

We e-mail these jokes and sometimes it says, at the end of the jokes, pass this on to 10 friends for your wishes to come true so we do. I am passing this on so you can read the ones you may have gotten or forgot. Perhaps you want to remember how you really can laugh. We remember those gut wrenching laughs where we find ourselves crying hysterically even for no other reason but to find that true rib or funny bone. I thank all my doctor friends who in their busy days get a chance to read and pass on the jokes. Don't forget the groaners as some call it, these are the jokes where your lips make that flat puckered look and that sound Ahhh.

The multitudes of those who will find themselves in cars, planes, offices, homes, and apartments for you here is the moment to jiggle your bellies. All good healthy laughs.

CHAPTER 1 REDNECK

REDNECK BIRTHIN'

In the back woods of Tennessee, a redneck's wife went into labor in the middle of the night, and the doctor was called out to assist in the delivery. Since there was noelectricity, the doctor handed the father-to-be a lantern and said, "Here, you hold this high so I can see what I am doing."

Soon the baby boy was brought into the world. "Whoa there" said the doctor, "Don't be in such a rush to put that lantern down. I think there's another one coming." Sure enough, within minutes, he had delivered a baby girl.

"Hold that lantern up, don't set it down, there's another one!" said the doctor.Within a few minutes he had delivered another baby girl.

"No,no, don't be in a hurry to put down that lantern!" It seems there's yet another one coming!" cried the doctor.

The redneck scratched his head in bewilderment, and asked the doctor, "Ya reckon the light's attractin 'em?"

OLD WEST

A three legged dog walks into a saloon in the Old West. He slides up to the bar and announces: "I'm looking fot the man who shot my paw."

MODERN GISMOS

Three men-one German, one Japanese and a hillbilly –were sitting naked in a sauna. Suddenly there was a beeping sound. The German Pressed his forearm and the beep stopped. The others looked at him questioningly. "That was my pager," he said. The Japanese fellow lifted his palm to his ear. When he finished, he explained, "That was my mobile phone. I have a microchip in my hand." The hillbilly felt decidedly low tech. Not to be outdone, he decided he had to do something just as impressive. He stepped out of the sauna and went to the bathroom. He returned with a piece of toilet paper hanging from his behind. The others raised their eyebrows and stared at him. The hillbilly finally said, " Well, will you look at that . I'm getting a FAX."

TWO REASONS WHY IT'S SO HARD TO SOLVE A REDNECK MURDER

1. All the DNA is the same.
2. There are no dental records.

HILLBILLY MEDICAL TERMS

Artery… The study of paintings.
Benign…. What you be after you be eight.
Bacteria…Back door to cafeteria.
Barium…What you do with dead folks.
Cauterize…Made eye contact with her.
Cesarean Section…A neighborhood in Rome
Cat scan…Searching for the cat. Cauterize.. Made eye contact with her.
Colic…. A sheep dog.
Coma.. A punctuation mark.
D&C… Where Washington is.
Dilate… To live longer than your kids do.
Enema…Not a friend.
Fester…Quicker than someone else.
Fibula… A small lie.
G.I.Series… World Series of military baseball.

Hangnail…What you hang your coat on.
Impotent…Distinguished ,well known.
Labor Pain… Getting hurt at work.
Morbid… a higher offer than I bid.
Nitrates… cheaper than day rates.
Medical Staff.. A doctor's cane, sometimes shown with a snake.
Node… I knew it.
Outpatient…A person who has fainted.
Pap Smear… A fatherhood test.
Pelvis… second cousin to Elvis
Post Operative…A letter carrier.
Recovery Room…Place to do upholstery.
Rectum…Dum near kilt him.
Secretion… Hiding something.
Tablet…A small table to change babies on.
Seizure…Roman emperor who lived in the Cesarean section.
Terminal Illness…Getting sick at the stain station.
Tumor … More then one.
Urine…Opposite of mine
Varicose… Nearby.
Hospital…The biggest building in town, other than Joe's feed
warehouse or Frank's lumber mill.

NUTS
What are the difference between Beer Nuts and Deer Nuts?
Beer Nuts are $1, and Deer Nuts are always under a buck.

YOU KNOW YOU'RE A REDNECK WHEN:
You take your dog for a walk and you both use the same
tree.
Your boat has not left the driveway in 15 years.
The Salvation Army declines your mattress.

You come back from the dump with more than you took.

You're been involved in a custody fight over a hunting dog.

You think a hot tub is a stolen indoor plumbing fixture.

You know how many bales of hay your car will hold.

You have a rag for a gas cap.

Your house doesn't have curtains but your truck does.

You wonder how service stations keep their restrooms so clean.

You consider your license plate personalized because your father made it.

You have a complete set of salad bowls and they all say Cool Whip on the side.

The biggest city you've ever been to is Wal-Mart.

You thought the Unibomber was a wrestler.

You've ever used you ironing board as a buffet table.

Somebody tells you that you've got something in your teeth and you take them out to see what it is.

ESTATE

The South Carolina redneck passed away and left his entire estate in trust for his widow but she can't touch it until she turns fourteen.

TV

What do you call reruns of "Hee Haw" in Mississippi? A documentary.

REDNECK ONE LINERS

How many rednecks does it take eat a 'possum? Two. One to eat, and one to watch out for traffic.

Why did God invent armadillos? So that Texas rednecks can have 'possum on a halfshell.

Arkansas State trooper pulls over a pickup truck on I-40. He says to the driver, "Got any ID?" The driver says, "Bout what?" A new law recently passed in North Carolina: When a couple gets divorced, they're still brother and sister.

What do you get when you have 32 rednecks in the same room? A full set of teeth.

What do you call an Alabama farmer with a sheep under each arm? A pimp.

Why do driver education classes and redneck schools use the car only on Mondays, Wednesdays, and Fridays? Because on Tuesday and Thursday this sex education class uses it.

What's the difference between a southern zoo in northern zoo? A southern zoo has a description of the animal in the front of the cage, along with the recipe.

What's the difference between a northern fairytale and a southern fairytale? A northern fairytale begins " Once upon a time..." A southern fairytale begins 'Y'all ain't gonna believe this shit..'

CHAPTER 2 RELIGIOUS

LITTLE CATHOLIC SCHOOL HUMOR

Two nuns. Sister Catherine and Sister Helen, are traveling through Europe in their car. They get to Transylvania and are stopped at a traffic light. Suddenly, out of nowhere, a tiny little Dracula jumps onto the hood of the car and hisses at them through the windshield. "Quick, quick," shouts Sister Catherine, "What shall we do?" "Turn the windshield wipers on. That will get rid of the abomination," says Sister Helen. Sister Catherine switches them on knocking little Dracula about, but he clings to the wiper blade and continues hissing at the nuns. "What shall I do now?" she shouts. "Switch on the windshield washer; I filled it up with Holy Water at the Vatican," says Sister Helen. Sister Catherine turns on the windshield washer. Dracula screams as the water burns his skin, but he still clings and continues hissing at the nuns. "Now what?" shouts Sister Catherine. "Show him your cross," says Sister Helen. "Now you're talking," says Sister Catherine. She opens the window and shouts "Get the F____ off the car!

FRIARS

These friars were behind on their belfry payments, so they opened up a small florist shop to raise funds. Since everyone liked to buy flowers from the men of God, a rival florist across town thought the competition was unfair. He asked the good fathers to close down, but they would not. He went back and begged the friars to close. They ignored him. So, the rival florist hired Hugh Mac Taggart, the roughest and most vicious thug in town to "persuade" them to close. Hugh beat up the friars and trashed their store, saying he'd be back if they didn't close up shop. Terrified, they did so, thereby proving that Hugh, and only Hugh, can prevent florist friars.

MAHATMA GANDHI

Mahatma Gandhi, as you know, walked barefoot most of the time, whichproduced an impressive set of calluses on his feet. He also ate very little,which made him rather frail. The odd diet he had made him suffer from bad breath. This made him... what? A supercalloused fragile mystic hexed by halitosis.

CHRISTMAS JOKE

Three men died on Christmas Eve and were met by Saint Peter at the pearly gates. "In honor of this holy season," Saint Peter said, "you must each possess something that symbolizes Christmas to get into heaven." The first man fumbled through his pockets and pulled out a lighter. He flicked it on. It represents a candle, he said. You may pass through the pearly gates Saint Peter said. The second man reached into his pocket and pulled out a set of keys. He shook them and said, "They're bells". Saint Peter said you may pass through the pearly gates. The third man started searching desperately through his pockets and finally pulled out a pair of women's panties. St. Peter looked at the man with a raised eyebrow and asked, "And just what do those symbolize?" The man replied, "They're Carols".

NATIVITY SCENE PROHIBITED

The Supreme Court ruled there cannot be a nativity scene in Washington, DC this Christmas. This isn't for any religious or constitutional reason, they simply have not been able to find three wise men and a virgin in the nation's capitol. There was no problem, however finding enough asses to fill the stable

HEAVEN'S GATE

On their way to get married, a young couple are involved in a fatal car accident. The couple find themselves sitting outside the Pearly Gates waiting for St. Peter to process them into Heaven. While waiting, they begin to wonder: Could they possibly get married in Heaven? When St. Peter shows up, they asked him. St. Peter says, "I don't know. This is the first time anyone has asked. Let me go find out," and he leaves. The couple sat and waited for an answer. . .. . .for a couple of months. While they waited, they discussed that IF they were allowed to get married in Heaven, SHOULD they get married, what with the eternal aspect of it all."What if it doesn't work?" they wondered, "Are we stuck together FOREVER?"After yet another month, St. Peter finally returns, looking somewhat bedraggled. "Yes," he informs the couple, "you CAN get married in Heaven.""Great!" said the couple, "But we were just wondering, what if things don't work out? Could we also get a divorce in Heaven?"St. Peter, red-faced with anger, slams his clipboard onto the ground."What's wrong?" asked the frightened couple."OH, COME ON!!" St. Peter shouts, "It took me three months to find a priest up here! Do you have ANY idea how long it'll take me to find a lawyer?

HEAVEN
AN HMO MANAGER GOES TO HEAVEN. .

Two doctors and an HMO manager died and lined up at the pearly gates for admission to heaven. St. Peter asked them to identify themselves. One doctor stepped forward and said, "I was a pediatric spine surgeon and helped kids overcome their deformities." St. Peter said, "You can enter."The second doctor said, "I was a psychiatrist. I helped people rehabilitate themselves." St. Peter also invited him in. The third applicant stepped forward and said, "I was an HMO manager. I helped people get cost-effective health care." St. Peter said, "You can come in, too."But as the HMO manager walked by, St. Peter added, "You can stay three days. After that, you can go to Hell."

CATHOLIC MATH

Little David, who was Jewish, was failing math. His parents tried everything. Tutors, mentors, flashcards, special learning centers, and nothing helped. As a last resort, someone told them to try a Catholic school. "Those nuns are tough" they said. David was soon enrolled at St. Mary's. After school on the very first day David ran through the door and straight to his room, without even kissing his mother hello. He started studying furiously, books and papers spread out all over his room. Right after dinner he ran upstairs without mentioning TV, and hit the books harder than before. His parents were amazed. This behavior continued for weeks, until report card day arrived. David quietly laid the envelope on the table, and went to his room. With great trepidation, his mother opened the report. David had gotten an A in math! She ran up to his room, threw her arms around him and asked, "David honey, how did this happen? Was it the nuns? "No!", said David. "On the first day of school when I saw that guy nailed to the plus sign, I knew they weren't fooling around!"

POPE'S BLESSINGS

The Pope was finishing his sermon. He ended it with the Latin phrase "Tuti Homini.".... Blessed be Mankind.A woman's rights group approached the Pope the next day to mention that he blessed all Mankind but not Womankind. The next day, after His sermon, the Pope concluded by saying, "Tuti Homini, et Tuti Femini."... Blessed be Mankind and Womankind. The next day a gay-rights group approached the Pope. They said they noticed that he blessed mankind and womankind, and asked if he could also bless gay people. The Pope said, "Of course." The next day the Pope concluded his sermon with, "Tuti Homini, et Tuti Femini, et Tuti Fruiti."

ONCE A BAPTIST---- ALWAYS A BAPTIST

John Smith was the only Protestant to move into a large Catholicneighborhood. On the first Friday of Lent, John was outside grilling a big juicy steak on his grill.

Meanwhile, all of his neighbors were eating cold tuna fish for supper. Thiswent on each Friday of Lent. On the last Friday of Lent, the neighborhoodmen got together and decided that something had to be done about John, hewas tempting them to eat meat each Friday of Lent, and they couldn't take it anymore. They decided to try and convert John to be a Catholic. They went over and talked to him and were so happy that he decided to join all of his neighbors and become a Catholic. They took him to Church, and the Priest sprinkled some water over him, and said, "You were born a Baptist, you were raised a Baptist, and now you are a Catholic."

The men were so relieved, now their biggest Lenten temptation was resolved. The next year's Lenten season rolled around. The first Friday of Lent came, and just at supper time, when the neighborhood was setting down to their tuna fish dinner, came the wafting smell of steak cooking on a grill. The neighborhood men could not believe their noses! WHAT WAS GOING ON? They called each other up and decided to meet over in John's yard to see if he had forgotten it was the first Friday of

Lent? The group arrived just in time to see John standing over his grill with a small pitcher of water. He was sprinkling some water over his steak on the grill, saying, "You were born a cow, you were raised a cow, and now you are a fish."

JEWISH HUTSPA

The optimist sees the bagel, the pessimist sees the hole.

If you can't say something nice,say it in Yiddish.

If it tastes good, it's probably not kosher.

Why spoil a good meal with a big tip?

WASPS leave and never say goodbye, Jews say goodbye and never leave.

Israel's the land of milk and honey, North London is the land of milk of Magnesia.

Never pay retail. It's always a bad hair day if you are bald. No one leaves the Jewish wedding hungry, but then again no one leaves with a hangover.

The high holidays have absolutely nothing to do with marijuana.

Always whisper the names of diseases.

If you don't eat, it will kill me.

Anything worth saying is worth repeating 1000 times.

Where there's smoke, there may be smoked salmon.

Never leave a restaurant empty-handed.

A bad matzoh ball makes a good paperweight.

Without Jewish mother's, who would need therapy?

Before you read the menu, read the prices.

There's a time in every man's life when he must stand up and tell his mother He is an adult. This usually happens at around 45.

According to Jewish dietary law, pork and shellfish maybe only eaten in Chinese restaurants.

If you're going to whisper at the movies, make sure it's loud enough for everyone to hear.

If you have to ask the price, you can't afford it. But if you can't afford it, make sure you tell everyone what you paid.

THE IRISH GIRL

An Irish girl went to London to work as a secretary and began sending home money and gifts to her parents. After a few years they asked her to come home for a visit, as her father was getting frail and elderly. She pulled up to the family home in a Rolls Royce and stepped out wearing furs and diamonds. As she walked into the house her father said "Hmmm they seem to be paying secretaries awfully well in London." The girl took his hands and said 'Dad, I've been meaning to tell you something for years but I didn't want to put it in a letter. I can't hide it from you any longer. I've become a prostitute." Her father gasped, put his hand on his heart and keeled over. The doctor was called but the old man had clearly lost the will to live. He was put to bed and the priest was called. As the priest began to administer Extreme Unction, with the mother and daughter weeping and wailing, the old man muttered weakly "I'm a goner killed by my own daughter! Killed by the shame of what you've become!" "Please forgive me", his daughter sobbed, 'I only wanted to have nice things! I wanted to be able to send you money and the only way I could do it was by becoming a prostitute." Brushing the priest aside, the old man sat bolt upright in bed smiling. "Did you say prostitute?..... I thought you said PROTESTANT!!'"

OLD CHINESE PROVERBS

Virginity like bubble, one prick, all gone.

Man with hand in pants feel cocky all day.

Foolish man give wife grand piano, wise man give wife upright organ.

Man who walk through airport turnstyle sideways going to Bangkok.

Baseball is wrong: man with four balls cannot walk.

Panties not best thing on Earth ! But next to best thing on Earth.

War not determined who is right, war determine who is left.

Wife who put husband in doghouse soon find him in cat house.

Man who stand on toilet is hMan who far tin church sit in own pew.

Crowded elevator smell different to midget.

HOLY WATER

How do get Holy Water?
You boil the Hell out of it.

WIFE DIED IN JERUSALEM

A man and his ever-nagging wife went on vacation to Jerusalem.

While they were there, the wife passed away The undertaker told the Husband, "You can have her shipped home for $5,000, or bury her here, in the Holy Land, for $150."

The man thought about it and told him to ship her home. The undertaker asked,"Why would you spend $5,000 to ship your wife home, when it would be wonderful to be buried here and you would spend only$150?"

The man replied,"Long ago a man died here, was buried here, and three days later he rose from the dead. I just can't take that chance."

CHURCHES IN LAS VEGAS

This may come as a surprise to those of you not living in Las Vegas, but there are more Catholic churches there than casinos. Not surprisingly, some worshipers at Sunday services will give casino chips rather than cash when the basket is passed. Since they get chips from so many different casinos, the churches have devised a method to process these offerings. The churches send all their collected chips to a nearby Franciscan Monastery for sorting and then the chips are taken to the casinos of origin and cashed in. This is done by the chip monks.

BATH IN HOLY WATER

It was time for Father John's Saturday night bath and the young nun, Sister Magdalene, had prepared the bath water and towels just the way the old nun had instructed.

Sister Magdalene was also instructed not to look at Father John's nakedness if she could help it, do whatever he told her to do, and pray.

The next morning the old nun asked Sister Magdalene how the Saturday night bath had gone.

'Oh, sister,' said the young nun dreamily, 'I've been saved.'

'Saved? And how did that come about?' asked the old nun.

'Well, when Father John was soaking in the tub, he asked me to wash him, and while I was washing him he guided my hand down between his legs where he said the Lord keeps the Key to Heaven.'

'Did he now?' said the old nun evenly.

Sister Magdalene continued, 'And Father John said that if the Key to Heaven fit my lock, the portals of Heaven would be opened to me and I would be assured salvation and eternal peace. And then Father John guided his Key to Heaven into my lock.'

'Is that a fact?' said the old nun even more evenly. 'At first it hurt terribly, but Father John said the pathway to salvation was often painful and that the glory of God would soon swell my heart with ecstasy. And it did, it felt so good being saved.'

'That wicked old Sod, said the old nun. 'He told me it was Gabriel's Horn, and I've been blowing it for 40 years!

THE BILLBOARD

I saw a billboard sign that said:
NEED HELP, CALL JESUS
1-800-005-3787
Out of curiosity, I did.
A Mexican showed up with a lawn mower.

PEARLY GATES OF HEAVEN

Once upon a time a woman died and went to heaven. When she reached the Pearly Gates she was met by St. Peter. She said, "Am I in heaven?"

He said, "Yes, you are at the Pearly Gates." "Do I get to come in?" asked the women.

St. Peter said, "Yes, if you can spell a word." "What word?" "Any word."

She said, "Ok, I'll spell love." She did and she was allowed to enter. A few minutes later, St. Peter approached her and said, "I have to leave for a minute. Would you wwatch the gate?" She looked astonished and said, " you want me to watch the gate?"

St. Peter said, "Yes."

She asked, "What do I do if someone comes up?" He replied, " Just what I did. Ask them to spell a word." As she stood looking around at all the beautiful sights in heaven, she saw a man walking toward the gates. As he drew closer, the woman recognized him. It was her husband. She was shocked! He walked up to the gates. "What happened?" the wife asked. "Well," the husband replied, "I was so upset after your funeral that on the way home I had an accident and died. Am I in heaven?" "You are at the Pearly Gates," she said. "Yes, but you have to spell a word," she said. "What word?" he asked. "Czechoslovakia," she replied.

MORE YEARS TO GO

A middle aged woman had a heart attack and was taken to the hospital. While on the operating room table she had a near death experience. Seeing god, she asked, "Is my time up?" God said, "No you have another 43 years, 2 months and 8 days to live."

Upon recovery, the woman decided to stay in the hospital and facelift, liposuction, and tummy tuck. She even had someone come and change the color of her hair. Since she had so much time to live, she figured she might as well make the most of it.

After her last operation, she was released from the hospital. While crossing the street on her way home, she was killed by an ambulance. Arriving in front of God , she demanded, "I thought you said I had another 40+ years? Why didn't you pull me form the path of the ambulance?" God replied, "I didn't recognize you.

THE BURGLAR

The burglar was creeping noiselessly through the darkened home, filling his bag with various valuables. As he reached his hand out to a box of jewelry, he heard a voice say,

"Jesus is watching you," Shaken, the burglar stopped. For a full minute he didn't dare breathe. Finally, he switched on his flashlight and carefully played it around the room, but saw nothing. Convinced that it must have been his imagination, he turned off the flash light and continued in his quest for another man's wealth, He was busily unhooking

A stereo set when he again heard, "Jesus is watching you." This time he nearly jumped out of his skin, he was so freaked out. Beads of sweat popped out on his face, and as he switched the light on again, the beam shook violently from his terror, He looked about the room, and noticed a bird cage in the corner. Upon closer inspection, he discovered a parrot in the cage. " Are you the one that spoke to me just now?" asked the burglar.

"Yes, I am," said the parrot. "Why did you say "Jesus is watching you?" Asked the man.

"Because I felt like you needed to be warned," replied the parrot. By the time, the man was over his fright and was more than a little irritated at this smart-mouthed parrot that had tried to scare the living daylights out of him. "What's your name?" Asked the burglar. "Moses," the parrot said. "Ha," the man guffawed. "What kind of people would name their parrot Moses?" The parrot exclaimed, "The same kind of people that would name their Rottweiler Jesus."

THE THREE POLITICIANS

Bill Clinton, Al gore and George Bush died and found themselves standing on the

Other side of the Jordan River, looking across at the promised land. The Archangel Michael was standing on the other side and shouted over to the three surprised Americans, "Contrary to what you have been taught, each of you will have to wade across the Jordan River." As Michael saw their perplexed looks, he reassured them by saying, "Don't worry. You will only sink proportionally according to your sins on earth. The more you have sinned the more you will sink into the water." The tree American sages of political lore looked at one another, trying to determine who shall be the first brave soul to cross the Jordan River. Finally George Bush volunteered to go first. Slowly he began to wade out into the river, and slowly the water began to get higher and higher, reaching to his waist. George began to sweat, thinking that all of his sins are coming back to haunt him. He was beginning to wonder if he would ever see the other side. Finally, after what seemed like an eternity, He began to emerge on the river's bank. As he ascended to the other side, he looked behind him to see which one of the other brave souls was going next. A shock of surprised registered on his face, as he saw Al gore almost in the middle of the river and only his ankles barely touching the water. He turned to Michael and exclaimed, "I know Al gore, Al gore is a friend of mine, and he has sinned much, much, more that that!" Before the Archangel Michael could reply, Al Gore shouted back, "I,m standing on Clinton's shoulders!"

RABBI MOISHE AND THE POPE

Several centuries ago, the Pope decreed that all the Jew had to leave Italy, or convert. There was, of course, a huge outcry from the Jewish community, so the Pope offered a deal. He would have a religious debate with a leader of the Jewish community. If the Jew won the debate, the Jews would be permitted to stay in Italy. If the Pope won, the Jews would have to leave. The Jewish community met and picked an aged Rabbi, Moishe, to represent them in the debate. Rabbi Moishe, however, could not speak Latin, and the Pope could speak Yiddish. So it was decided that theirs would be a "silent" debate.

On the day of the great debate, the Pope and Rabbi Moishe sat opposite each other for a full minute before the Pope raised his hand and showed three fingers. Rabbi Moishe looked back and raised one finger. Next, the Pope waved his finger around his head.

Rabbi Moishe pointed to the ground where he sat. The Pope then brought out a communion wafer and chalice of wine. Rabbi Moshe pulled out an apple. With that, the Pope stood up and said, "I concede the debate. This man has bested me. The Jews can stay." Later, the Cardinals gathered around the Pope asking him what had happened.

The Pope said, "First I held up three fingers to represent the Trinity. He responded by holding up one finger to remind me that there was still one God common to both our religions. Then I waved my finger around me to show him that God was all around us. He responded by pointing to the ground to show that God was also right here with us. I pulled out the wine and the wafer to show that God absolves us of our sins. He pulled out an apple to remind me of original sin. He had an answer for everything. What could we do?" Meanwhile , the Jewish community crowded around Rabbi Moishe. "What happened?" they asked. "Well," said Rabbi Moishe, "First he said to me, You Jews have three days to get out of here!" So I said to him, " Up yours!" then he tells me the whole city would be cleared of Jews. So I said to him, "Listen here, Mr. Pope, the Jews will stay right here!" "And then?" asked a woman "Who knows?" said Rabbi Moishe. "He took out his lunch, so I took out mine."

HEBREW ARCHEOLOGISTS

A group of archeologists were exploring when they came upon a cave.

Written across the wall of the cave were the following symbols, in this order of appearance: a woman, a donkey, a shovel, a fish, and a Star of David.

They decided that this was a unique find and the writings were at least three-thousand years old. They chopped out the piece of stone and had it brought to the museum where archaeologists from all over the world came to study the ancient symbols. They held a huge meeting after months of conferences to discuss the meaning of the markings. The president of the society stood up and pointed at the first drawing and said, "This looks like a woman. We can judge that this race was family oriented and held women in high esteem. You can also tell they were intelligent, as the next symbol resembles a donkey, so, they were smart enough to have animals help them till the soil. The next drawing looks like a shovel of some sort, which means they even had tools to help them.

Even further proof of their high intelligence is the fish which means that if a famine had hit the earth, whereby the food didn't grow, they would take to the sea for food. The last symbol appears to be the Star of David which means they were evidently Hebrews.

The audience applauded enthusiastically. Suddenly a little old Jewish man stood up in the back said,"Idiots! Hebrew is read from right to left." It says, "Holy Mackerel, dig the Ass on that Woman."

SONG LEARNED

A child came back from Junior Church one Sunday and told his mother htat they had learned a new song about a cross-eyed bear named "Gladly."

It took his mother a while before she realized that the hymn was "Gladly, the Cross I'd Bear."

FAITHFUL DOG

A man and his dog were walking along a road. The man was enjoying the scenery, when suddenly occurred to him that he was dead. He remembered dying and that his faithful dog had been dead for many years. He wondered where the road was leading them. After a while, they came to a high , white stone wall along one side of the road. It looked like fine marble . As he reached the wall, he saw a magnificent gate in the arch and the street that led to the gate was made from pure gold. He and the dog walked toward the gate; as he got closer, he saw a man at a desk to one side. When he was close enough, he called out, "Excuse me, where are we?" " This is heaven, sir," the man answered. "Wow! Would you happen to have some water? We have traveled far," the man said.

"Of course, sir. Come right in and I'll have some ice water brought right up."

The man gestured, and the gate began to open. "Can my friend," gesturing toward his

dog, "Come in too?" the traveler asked. "I'm sorry, sir , but we don't accept pets."

The man thought a moment, remembering all the years this dog remained loyal to him and then turned back toward the road and continued the way he had been going.

After another long wask, he came to a plain dirt road which let through a farm gate that looked as if it had never been closed. There was no fence. As he approached the gate, he saw a man inside, leaning against a tree and reading a book. "Excuse me!" he called to the reader. "Do you have any water? We have traveled far." "Yes, sure there's a faucet over there." The man pointed to a place that couldn't be seen from outside the gate. "Come on in and help yourself." " How about my friend here?" the traveler gestured to his dog. " There should be a bowl by the faucet, he is welcome to share." They went through the gate, and sure enough, there was an old-fashioned faucet with a bowl beside it. The traveler filled the bowl, took a long drink himself, then gave some to the dog. When they were full, he and the dog walked back toward the man who was standing by the tree waiting for them. "What do you call this place?" the traveler asked. "This is heaven," was the answer. "Well, that's confusing," traveler said. "The man down the road said that was heaven too." "Oh, you mean the place with the gold street and pearly gates? Nope. That's hell." "Doesn't it make you mad for them to use your name like that?"

"No. We're just happy that they screen out the folks who'd leave their best friends behind in exchange for material things."

PREACHER

A young doctor moved out to a small community to replace the aging doctor there. The older doctor suggested that the younger doctor accompany him as he made his house calls so that the people of the community could become accustomed to him. At the first house they visited, the younger doctor listened intently as the older doctor and an older lady discussed the weather, their grandchildren and the latest church bulletin. After some time, the older doctor asked his patient how she had been feeling. "I've been a little sick to my stomach," she replied. "Well," said the older physician,"You've probably been over doing it a bit with the fresh fruit. Why don't you cut back on the amount of fresh fruit you eat and see if that helps." As they left the house, the younger doctor asked how the older doctor had reached his diagnosis so quickly. "You didn't even examine that woman," the younger doctor stated. "I didn't have to," the elder physician explain. "You noticed that I dropped my stethoscope on the floor in there. Well when I bent over to pick it up, I looked around and noticed a half dozen banana peels in the trash can.

That is probably what has been making her ill." "That's pretty sneaky," commented the younger doctor. "Do you mind if I try it at the next house?" "I don't suppose it could hurt anything," the elder physician replied. At the next house, the two doctors visited with an elderly window. They spent several minutes discussing the weather and grandchildren and the latest church bulletin. After several minutes, the younger doctor asked the widow how she had been feeling lately. "I've felt terribly run down lately, " the widow replied. " I just don't have as much energy as I used to ." "You've probably been doing too much work for the church," the younger doctor suggested without even examining his patient. "Perhaps you should ease up a bit and see if that helps." As they left, the elder physician said, "Your diagnosis is probably right, but do you mind telling me how you came to that conclusion?" "Sure," replied the younger doctor. "Just like you, I dropped my stethoscope on the floor. When I bent down to pick it up, I looked around and there was the preacher hiding under the bed!"

CASTRO IN HEAVEN

Fidel dies and goes to heaven. When he gets there, St. Peter tells him that he is not on the list and that no way, no how, does he belong in heaven.

Fidel must go to hell. So Fidel goes to hell where Satan gives him a hearty welcome and tells him to make himself at home. Then Fidel notices that he left his luggage in heaven and tells Satan, who says, "No problem, I'll send a couple of devils to get your stuff."

When the little devils get to heaven they find the gates are locked. St. Peter is having lunch, and they start debating what to do. Finally one comes up with the idea that they should go over the wall and get the luggage. As they are climbing the wall, two little angels see them, and one angel says to the other, "My God! Fidel has been in hell no more than ten minutes and we're already getting refugees..!"

JEWISH FATHER PROBLEM

A Jewish Father's was concerned about his son who was about a year away from his Bar Mitzvah, but was sorely lacking in his knowledge of the Jewish faith. To remedy this, he sent his son to Israel to experience his heritage firsthand. A year later, the young man returned home, saying, "Father, thank you for sending me to the land of our Fathers." The son said. 'It was a wonderful and enlightening experience; however, I must confess that while in Israel, I converted to Christianity." "Oi vey," replied the old man, "what have I done?" So, in the tradition of the patriarchs, he went to his best friend and sought his advice and solace. 'It is amazing that you should come to me with this question," said his friend, "I, too sent my son to Israel, and he returned a Christian." So, in the traditions of the Patriarchs, they went to see the Rabbi. "It is amazing that you should come to me," said the Rabbi. "I, too sent my son to Israel and HE returned as a Christian. What is happening to our sons?" Brothers, we must take this to the Lord," said the Rabbi. So, they fell to their knees and began to wail and pour out their hearts to the Almighty. As they prayed, the clouds above opened up and a mighty voice boomed out, 'Amazing that you should come to me with his problem. I, too , sent My Son to Israel.

PASTOR'S BUSINESS CARD

A new pastor was visiting in the homes of his parishioners. At one house it seemed

Obvious that someone was at home, but no answer came to his repeated knocks at the door. Therefore, he took out a business card and wrote "Revelation 3:20" on the back of it and stuck it in the door. When the offering was processed the following Sunday, he found that his card had been returned. Added to it was this cryptic message,

"Genesis 3:10." Reaching for his Bible to check out the citation, he broke up in gales of laughter. Revelation 3:20 begins "Behold I stand at the door and knock."Genesis 3:10 reads, " I heard your voice in the garden and I was afraid for I was naked."

HAPTER 3 ETHNIC: AMERICAN, FRENCH, GERMAN, IRISH, ETC...

ESKIMOS

Two Eskimos sitting in a kayak were chilly, but when they lit a fire in the craft, it sank. This proves once again that you can't have your kayak and heat it too.

What do Eskimos get from sitting on the ice too long? Polaroids.

INDIAN WINTERS

It was autumn, and the Native American Indians on the remote reservation asked their new Chief if the winter was going to be cold or mild. Since he was a Chief in a modern society he had never been taught the old secrets, and when he looked at the sky, he couldn't tell what the weather was going to be. Nevertheless, to be on the safe side, he replied to his tribe that the winter was indeed going to be cold and that the members of the village should collect wood to be prepared. But also being a practical leader, after several days he got an idea. He went to the phone booth, called the National Weather Service and asked, "Is the coming winter going to be cold?"It looks like this winter is going to be quite cold indeed," the Meteorologist at the weather service responded. So the Chief went back to his people and told them to collect even more wood in order to be prepared. One week later he called the National Weather Service again. "Is it going to be a very cold winter?" he asked. "Yes," the man at National Weather Service again replied, "it's going to be a very cold winter."The Chief again went back to his people and ordered them to collect every scrap of wood they could find.

Two weeks later he called the National Weather Service again. "Are you absolutely sure that the winter is going to be very cold?"Absolutely," the man replied. "It looks like it's going to be one of the coldest winters ever.""How can you be so sure?" the Chief asked. The weatherman replied, "The Indians are collecting firewood like crazy."

MEXICAN MURDER INVESTIGATION

Two Mexican detectives were investigating the murder of Juan Gonzalez.

"How was he killed?" asked one detective.

"With a golf gun," the other detective replied.

"A golf gun?! What is a golf gun?"

"I don't know. But it sure made a hole in Juan."

DELIVER TO VERA CRUZ MEXICO

Concerning the great ship"Titanic." Most people don't know that in 1912, Hellman's Mayonnaise was manufactured in England. The Titanic was carrying 12,000 jars of the condiment, scheduled for delivery in Vera Cruz, Mexico which was to be the next port of call for the great shipafter New York City. The people of Mexico eagerly awaited the first delivery and was very upset at the news of the sinking. So much so that they declared a national day of mourning which they still observe. It is known, of course, as Sinko de Mayo.

What do you call four bullfighters in quicksand? Quattro Sinko.

THE RED SPOT

For centuries, Hindu women have worn a red spot on their foreheads. We have naively thought it had something to do with their religion. The true story has just been revealed by the Indian Embassy in Washington. When one of these women gets married, on her wedding night, the husband scratches off the red spot to see if he has won a convenience store, as gas station, or a motel in Florida.

IN SEARCH OF WATER

An Arab was walking through the Sahara desert, desperate for water, when he saw something, far off in the distance. Hoping to find water, he walked towards the image, only to find a little old Jewish man sitting at a card table with a bunch of neckties laid out on it.

The Arab asked, "Please, I'm dying of thirst, can I have some water?"

The man replied, 'I don't have any water, but why don't you buy a tie?"

Here's one that goes nicely with your robes."

The Arab shouted, "I don't want a tie, you idiot, I need water!"

"OK, don't buy a tie. But to show you what a nice guy I am, I'll tell you that Over that hill there, about 4 miles, is a nice restaurant. Walk that way, they'll give you all the water you want."

The Arab disappeared. Three hours later the Arab came crawling back to where the Man was sitting behind his card table. He said 'I told you, about 4 miles over that hill. Couldn't You find it?" The Arab rasped "I found it all right Your brother wouldn't let me in without a tie.

ITALIAN WAYS

What would you call it when an Italian has one arm shorter than the other?

A speech impediment.

NATIONAL ANTHEM

What is the Cuban national anthem?

Row, Row, Row your boat.

AMERICAN VARIATIONS

What's the difference between a Northern fairy tale and Southern fairy tale?

A Northern fairy tale begins "Once upon a time."

A Southern fairy tale begins "Y'all ain't gonna believe this"

PILGRIMS

Why did Pilgrim's pants always fall down?

Because they wore their belt buckle on their hats.

What goes clop, clop, clop, bang, bang, bang, clop, clop, clop?

An Amish drive by shooting.

IT IS ALL IN HOW YOU SAY IT

An Italian, a Scotsman and a Chinese are hired at a construction site. The foreman points out a huge pile of sand. He says to the Italian guy, "You're in charge of sweeping." To the Scotsman he says, "You're in charge of shoveling." To the Chinese guy, "You're in charge of supplies."

He then says, "Now, I have to leave for a little while. I expect you guys to make a dent in that there pile of sand." So when the foreman returns, after being away for a couple hours, the pile of sand is untouched. He asks the Italian, "Why didn't you sweep any of it?" The Italian replies, "I no hava no broom. You said a to the Chinese-a fella that he asa in a charge of supplies, but he hasa disappeared and I no coulda finda him nowhere." Then the foreman turns to the Scotsman and says, and you, I thought I told you to shovel this pile." The Scotsman replies, "Aye, that ye did laddie, boot ah couldnay get meself a shovel!" Ye left th' Chinese gadgie in chairge of supplies, boot ah couldnay fin'him neither." The foreman is really angry now. He storms off toward the pile of sand to look for the Chinese guy. Just then, the Chinese leaps out from behind the pile of sand and yells…"Supplies!!!"

DESERTED ISLANDS

On a group of beautiful deserted islands in the middle of nowhere the following people are stranded:

Two Italian men and one Italian woman
Two French men and one French woman
Two German men and one German woman
Two Greek men and one Greek woman
Two English men and one English woman
Two Bulgarian men and one Bulgarian woman
Two Japanese men and one Japanese woman
Two Chinese men and one Chinese woman
Two Irish men and one Irish woman

One month later on these absolutely stunning deserted islands in the middle of nowhere the following things have occurred:

One Italian man killed the other Italian man for the Italian woman.

The two French men and the French woman are living happily together in a ménage-a trios.

The two German men have a strict weekly schedule of alternating visits with the German woman.

The two Greek men are sleeping with each other and the Greek woman is cleaning and cooking for them.

The two English men are waiting for someone to introduce them to the English woman.

The two Bulgarian men took one long look at the endless ocean and another long look at the Bulgarian woman and started swimming.

The two Japanese have faxed Tokyo and are awaiting instructions.

The two Chinese men have set up a pharmacy, liquor store, restaurant, laundry, and have gotten
the woman pregnant in order to supply employees for their store.

The two American men are contemplating the virtues of suicide because the American woman keeps on complaining about her body the true nature of feminism, how she can do everything they can do , the necessity of fulfillment , the equal division of household chores, how sand and palm trees make her look fat, how her last boyfriend respected her opinion and treated her nicer then they do, and how her relationship with her mother is improving, and how at least the taxes are low and it isn't raining.

The two Irish men divided the island into North and South and set up a distillery. They do not remember if sex is in the picture because it gets sort of foggy after the first few liters of coconut whiskey. But they're satisfied because at least the English aren't having any fun.

CHIEF SAMURAI

Once upon a time a powerful Emperor of the Rising Sun advertised for a new Chief Samurai.

After a year, only three applied for the job: a Japanese, a Chinese and a Jewish Samurai.

"Demonstrate your skills!" commanded the Emperor.

The Japanese samurai stepped forward, opened a tiny box and released one fly. He drew his samurai sword and Swoosh! The fly fell to the floor neatly divided in two pieces!

"What a feat!" said the Emperor. "Number two Samurai, show me what you can do.

The Chinese samurai smiled confidently, stepped forward and opened a tiny box, releasing one fly. He drew his samurai sword and Swoosh! Swoosh! The fly fell to the floor neatly divided into four pieces! "That is skill!" nodded the Emperor. "How are you going to top that, Number three Samurai?" "Number Three samurai" stepped forward, opened a tiny box releasing one fly, drew his samurai sword and Swooooosh!, flourished his sword so mightily that a gust of wind blew through the room. But the fly was still buzzing around! In disappointment, the Emperor said, "What kind of skill is that? The fly isn't dead." "Dead, schmead," replied the Jewish samurai.

"Dead is easy. I circumcised him!"

INSTRUCTIONS – ITALIAN ACCENT READ OUTLOUD

One day ima gonna Malta to bigga hotel. Ina Morning I go down to eat breakfast. I tella waitress I wanna two pissis toast. She brings me only one piss. I tella her I want two piss. She say go to the toilet . I say you no understand. I wanna to piss onna my plate. She say you better not piss onna your plate, you sonna ma bitch. I don't even know the lady and she call me sonna ma bitch. Later I go to eat at the bigga restaurant. The waitress brings me a spoon and knife but no fock. I talla her I wanna fock. She tell me everyone wanna fock. I tell her you no understand. I wanna fock on the table. She say you better no fock on the table, you sonna ma bitch. I don't even know the lady and she call me sonna ma bitch. So I go back to my room inna hotel and there is no shits onna my bed. Call the manager and tella him I wanna shit. He tell me to go to toilet. I say you no understand. I wanna shit on my bed. He say you better not shit onna bed, you sonna ma bitch. I don't even know the man and he call me sonna ma bitch. I go to the checkout and the man at the desk say:"Peace on you." I say piss on you too, yo sonna ma bitch , I gonna back to Italy.

BARN

A Hindu, a Jew and Castro were in a far away village having a hard time finding a place to sleep, they finally found an inn, but there was only 1 room available with 2 beds. They were told that one of them could sleep in the barn. The Hindu said, "Don't worry, I'll sleep in the barn". Five minutes later there was a knock on the door. "Who is it?" "It's me, the Hindu, there's a cow in the barn and since it's a sacred animal I won't sleep in the same room." The Jew then offered to go to the barn. Five minutes later there was a knock at the door. "Who is it?" "It's me, the Jew, there's a pig in the barn and I find that animal disgusting, so I just can't sleep next to it." Castro said, "No problem, I'll sleep in the barn". Five minutes later that was a knock on the door.
"Who is it?" "Mooo, Oink, Oink…"

LEARN CHINESE IN 5 MINUTES
Read out loud.
Ah Tink Yu Fa Ni!

He's cleaning his automobile.
Wa shing Ka.

This is a tow away zone.
No Pah King.

Is there a fugitive here?
Hu Yu Hai Ding?

Small Horse.
Tai Ni Po Ni.

Your price is too high!!!
Na Bai Nut Ding!!!

Did you go to the beach?
Wai Yu So Tan?

I bumped into a coffee table.
Ai Bang Mai Ni.

It's very dark in here.
Wai So Dim?

Has your flight been delayed?
Hao Long Wei Ting?

I thought you were on a diet.
Wai Yu Mun Ching?

They have arrived.
Hai Dei Kum.

Your body odor is offensive.
Yu Stin Ki Pu.

I got this for free
Ai No Pei.

You know lyrics to the Macarena?
Wai Yu Sing Dum Song?

Stay out of sight.
Lei Lo.

IMMIGRATION

I met a Chinese man who told me his name was Abe Schwartz. I asked him if he was Jewish

For which he replied no. "How did you get that name, did your mother marry a Jewish man?"

"Of course not! What happened was, when I came to this country and standing on the immigration line the man in front of me was named Abe Schwartz. When it came my turn,

They asked me my name and I said Sem Ting."

CHINESE PROVERBS

Passionate kiss like spider's web, soon lead to undoing of fly.

Virginity like bubble, one prick all gone.

Man who run in front of car get tired.

Man who run behind car get exhausted.

Man with hand in pocket feel cocky all day.

Foolish man give wife grand piano, wise man give wife upright organ.

Man who walk through airport turnstile sideways going to Bangkok.

Man with one chopstick go hungry.

Man who scratch ass should not bite fingernails.

Men who eat many prunes get good run for money.

Baseball wrong: man with four balls cannot walk.

Panties not best thing on earth button next to best thing on earth.

War not determine who is right, war determine who was left.

Wife who put husband in doghouse will soon find him in cat house.

Man who fight with wife all day get no piece at night.

It takes many nails to build crib but one screw to fill it.

Men who drive like Hell bound to get there.

Men who stand on toilet is high on pot.

Men who live in glass house should change clothes in basement.

Men who fish another man's well often catch crabs.

Man who fart in church sit in own pew.

Crowded elevators smell different to midget.

ETHNIC ONE LINERS

Where does an Irish family go on vacation? A different bar.

To hear about the Chinese couple that had a retarded baby? They named him Su Ting Wong.

What would you call it when an Italian has one arm shorter than the other? A speech impediment.

Why aren't there any Puerto Ricans on Star Trek? Because they're not going to work in the future either.

Did you hear about the dyslexic Rabbi? He walks around saying, "Yo."

CHAPTER 4 MEDICAL DENTAL AND SCIENCE

NEW DRUGS...

DAMITOL

Take 2 and the rest of the world can go to hell for up to 8 hours

ST. MOM'S WORT

Plant extract that treats mom's depression by rendering preschoolers unconscious for up to six hours.

EMPTYNESTROGEN

Highly effective suppository that eliminates melancholy by enhancing th memory of how awful they were as teenagers and how you couldn't wait until they moved out.

PEPTOBIMBO

Liquid silicone for single women. Two full cups swallowed before an evening out increases breast size, decreases intelligence, and improves flirting.

DUMEROL

When taken with Peptobimbo,can cause dangerously low I.Q. causing enjoyment of country western music

FLIPITOR

Increases life expectancy of commuters by controlling road rage and the urge to flip off other drivers.

MENICILLIN

Potent antiboyotic for older women. Increases resistance to such lines as, "You make me want to be a better person..can we get naked now?"

BUYAGRA

Injectable stimulant taken prior to going shopping. Increases potency and duration of spending spree

Extra Strength BUY-ONE-AL

When combined with Buyagra can cause an indiscriminate buying frenzy so severe the victim may even come home with a Donnie Osmone CD or a book by Dr. Laura.

JACKASSPIRIN

Relieves headache caused by a man who can't remember your birthday, anniversary or phone number.

ANTI-TALKSIDENT

A spray carried in a purse or wallet to be used on anyone too eager to share their life stories with total strangers.

SEXCEDRIN

More effective than Excedrine in treating the , "Not now, dear , I have a headache," syndrome.

RAGAMET

When administered to a husband, provides the same irritation as ragging on him all weekend, saving the wife the time and trouble of doing it herself.

ANTIBOYOTICS

When administered to teenage girls, is highly effective in improving grades, freeing up phone lines, and reducing money spent on make-up.

PATIENT TO DOCTOR

Patient comes to office and is finally seated in the treatment room And the doctor walks in. The patient says I came to the office Clean shaven.

TRIBAL MEDICINE

A young Native American women went for her first ever physical exam.

After checking all her vitals and running the usual tests the doctor said, "Well, Running Doe, you are in fine health. I could find no problems. I did notice one abnormality, however."

"Oh, what is that, Doctor?"

"Well you have no nipples."

"None of the people in my tribe have nipples," she replied.

"That is amazing" said the doc. "I'd like to write this up for The New England Journal of Medicine if you don't mind."

She said, "Okay."

"First of all" asked the doc, "How many people are in your tribe?"

She answered,"Approximately 500."

"And what is the name all of your tribe?" asked the doc.

Running Doe Replied, "We're called The Indian Nippleless Five Hundred."

PUBLIC SCHOOL TEACHER ARRESTED

New York

A public school teacher was arrested today at John F. Kennedy international Airport as he attempted to board a flight while in possession of a ruler, a protractor, a set square, slide rule and a calculator.

At a morning press conference, Atty. Gen. Alberto Gonzales said he believes the man is a member of the notorious Al-Gebra movement. He did not identify the man, who has been charged by the FBI with carrying weapons of math instruction.

"Al-Gebra is a problem for us," Gonzalez said. "They desire solutions by means and extremes, and sometimes go off on tangents in search of obsolete values. They use secret code names like 'x' and 'y' and refer to themselves as 'unknowns', but we have determined they belong to a common denominator of the axis of medieval and coordinates in every country. As the Greek philanderer Isosceles used to say, "There are three sides to every angle."

When asked to comment on the arrest, President Bush said, "If God had wanted us to have better weapons math instruction He would have given us more fingers and toes."

White House aides told reporters they cannot recall a more intelligent or profound statement by the President.

MEDICAL TEST

A man came in for chemo radiation and after the treatment the doctor said, "No
you can be called Chemosabe."

DRUGSTORE COMPUTER

One day, in line at the company cafeteria, Jack says to Mike behind him,

"My elbow hurts like hell. I guess I better see a doctor."

"Listen, you don't have to spend that kind of money," Mike replies.

"There's a diagnostic computer it the drugstore at the corner. Just give it a urine sample and the computer'll tell you what's wrong and what to do about it. It takes ten seconds and costs ten dollars. A hell of a lot cheaper than a doctor."

So Jack deposits a urine sample in a small jar and takes it to the drugstore. He deposits
ten dollars, and the computer lights up and asks for the urine sample. He pours the sample into the slot and waits. Ten seconds later, the computer ejects a printout:

You have tennis elbow. Soak your arm in warm water and avoid heavy activity. It will improve in two weeks.

That evening while thinking how amazing this new technology was, Jack began wondering if the computer could be fooled. He mixed some tap water, a stool sample
From his dog, urine samples from his wife and daughter, and masturbated into a mixture for good measure. Jack hurries back to the drugstore, eager to check the results. He deposits ten dollars, pours in his concoction, and waits the results. The computer prints the following:

1. Your tap water is too hard. Get a water softener.

2. Your dog has ringworm. Bathe him with anti-fungal shampoo.

3. Your daughter has a cocaine habit. Get her to rehab.

4. Your wife is pregnant.. twins girls. They aren't yours. Get a lawyer.

5. If you don't stop playing with yourself, your elbow will never get better.

CELLULAR DEVELOPMENT

All babies start out with the same number of raw cells which, over nine months, develop into a complete female baby. The problem occurs when cells are instructed by the little chromosomes to make a male baby instead. Because there are only so many cells to go around, the cells necessary to develop a male's reproductive organs have to come from cells already assigned elsewhere in the female. Recent tests have shown that these cells are removed from the communication center of the brain, migrate lower in the body and develop into male sexual organs. If you visualize a normal brain to be similar to a full deck of cards, this means that males are born a few cards short, so to speak. And some of their cards are in their shorts. This difference between the male and female brain manifests itself in various ways. Little girls will tend to play things like house or learn to read. Little boys, however, will tend to do things like placing a bucket over their heads and running into walls. Little girls will think about doing things before taking any action. Little boys will just punch or kick something and will look surprised if someone asks them why they just punched their little brother who was half asleep and looking other way. This basic cognitive difference continues to grow until puberty, when the hormones kick into action and the trouble really begins. After puberty, not only the size of the male and female's brain differs, but the center of thought also differs. Women think with their heads. Male thoughts often originate lower in their bodies where their ex-brain cells reside. Of course, the size of this problem varies from man to man. In some men only a

small number of brain cells migrate and they are left with nearly full mental capacity but they tend to be rather dull, sexually speaking. Such men are known in medical term as "Engineers." Other men suffer larger brain cell relocations. These men are medically referred to as "Lawyers." A small number of men suffer massive brain cell migration to their groins. These men are usually referred to as …"Mr. President."

DINING OUT

An elderly man and his wife were dinging at a restaurant. After the man received his food he carefully cut his portion in half, and poured exactly half of his drink into another cup. Then he gave these to his wife. Their waitress noticed that the old lady was not eating her half and said, "That's so sweet that you share the meal, but why aren't you eating?" The old lady said, "I'm waiting for the teeth!"

CAST YOUR VOTE

Recently, when a hospital panel, made up of doctor's was asked to vote on adding a new wing to the hospital, this is what happened...

The allergist voted to scratch it.

The dermatologists preferred no rash moves.

The neurologists thought the administration had a lot of nerve.

The obstetricians stated they were laboring under a misconception.

The ophthalmologists considered the idea short-sighted.

The parasitologists said, "well if you encyst."

The pathologists yelled, "over my dead body."

The pediatricians said, "grow up."

The proctologists said, "we are in errears."

The psychiatrists thought it was madness.

The surgeons decided to wash their hands of the whole thing.

The radiologists could see right through it.

The internists thought it was hard pill to swallow.

The plastic surgeons said, "this puts a whole new face on the matter."

The podiatrists thought it was a big step forward.

The urologists felt the scheme wouldn't hold water.

The anesthesiologists didn't have the heart to say no.

The cardiologists didn't have the heart to say no.

The new wing never made it.

VD

An American tourist goes on a trip to China. While in China, he is very sexually promiscuous. A week after arriving back home in the States, he awakes one morning to find his dick, covered with bright green and purple spots. Horrified, he immediately goes to see a doctor. The doctor, never having seen anything like this before, orders some tests and tells the man to return in two days, for the results. The man returns a couple of days later and the doctor says, "I've got bad news for you . You've got Mongolian VD. It's rare and almost unheard of here. We know very little about it." The man looks a little relieved and says "Well, give me a shot or something and fix me up," doc.

The doctor answers "I'm sorry, there's no known cure, We're going to have to amputate your penis." The man screams in horror, "Oh no! I want a second opinion!" The doctors replies, "Well it's your choice. Go ahead if you want , but surgery is your only choice."

The next day, the man seeks out a Chinese doctor, figuring that he'll know more about the disease. The Chinese doctor examines his dick, and proclaims "Ah yes, Mongolian VD. Velly lare disease." The syas to the doctor, "Yeah, yeah, I already know that, but what can you do? My American doctor wants to operate and amputate my penis!"

The Chinese doctor shakes his head and laughs, "Stipid Amellican doctor! Amellican doctor, always want to opulate. Make more money, that way. No need to opulate!"

"Oh thank God!" the man replies. "Yes" says the Chinese doctor, "You no worry! Wait two weeky. Dick fall off by self!"

MEDICAL ONE LINERS

He's not dead, he's electroenchephalographically challenged.
It was recently discovered that research causes cancer in rats.

HUNTING

A group of doctors go duck hunting for the first time. The family practitioner looks through the site, aims and says, "Well, I think there is something out there, but I better get another opinion.?

The internist takes the rifle, looks, and says, "I see something that is flying, but I'm not sure what it is. I better make a referral."

The neurologist takes the rifle, looks, and says, "Hmmm, it may be ducks, but to be sure,
I better get some tests."

The psychiatrist then looks through the rifle and says, "Vell, zay look like ducks, zay act like ducks, but I don't know if zay zink zay are ducks. I zink I better get a consult."

The surgeon picks up the rifle, points and fires all over the sky. "Blam, blam, blam, blam,!" All sorts of things fall from the sky and land at his feet. The surgeon point to them and says to the pathologist, "Make sure they're ducks!"

PSYCH WARD

There was this man in a mental hospital. All day he would put his ear to the wall and listen. The doctor would watch this guy do this day after day. The doctor finally decided to put his ear up to the wall and listened. He heard nothing. He turned to the mental patient and said, "I don't hear anything." The mental patient said, "Yeah, I know. It's been like that for months!"

WHO MAKES THE BEST PATIENT

Five surgeons are discussing who makes the best patients to operate on.

The first surgeon says, "I like to see accountants on my operating table, because when you open them up, everything inside is numbered."

The second responds, "Yeah, but you should try electricians! Everything inside them is color coded." The third surgeon says, "No, I really think librarians are the best; everything inside them is in alphabetical order!" The fourth surgeon chimes in: "You know, I like construction workers, those guys always understand when you have a few parts left over at the end, and when the job takes longer than you said it would."

The fifth surgeon shut them all up when he observed: "You're all wrong. Politicians are the easiest to operate on. There's no guts, no heart, and no spine, and the head and butt are interchangeable."

10 SIGNS YOU NEED A NEW DOCTOR

He calls you at two in the morning "Just to talk."

Instead of rubber surgical gloves he wears all the mitts.

He keeps accidentally referring to himself as " the defendant."

After examining you, he says, "Now do me."

He thinks Eastern medicine was developed in Long Island.

He keeps accidentally referring to your legs as "drumsticks."

His examination room is room 201 at the No-Tell Motel.

He introduces you to the anesthesiologist, "Doctor Jim Beam."

Before surgery, he asks if you want this "to go."

He tries to color your x-rays with crayons.

USEFUL ENGLISH SYSTEM CONVERSION UNITS

Ratio of an igloos circumference to its diameter: Eskimo Pi.

2.4 statute miles of intravenous surgical tubing at Yale University

Hospital: 1 I.V. League.

2000 pounds of Chinese soup: Won Ton.

Time it takes to said 220 yards at 1 nautical mile per hour: Knot-fer-long. 365 ¼ days of drinking low-calorie beer because its less filling: 1 lite year.

1000 grams of wet socks: 1 leterhosen.

Weight an evangelist carries with God: 1 Billigram.

Time between slipping on a peel and smacking the pavement: Bananosecond.

2000 mocking birds: 2 kilomockingbirds

100 senators: Not 1 Decision.

CYNIC'S MEDICAL DICTIONARY TERMS

Artificial insemination: Procreation without recreation.

Bookcase: A piece of furniture used in America to house bowling trophies and Elvis collectibles.

Bulimia: Wretched excess.

Dentures: Two rows of artificial ivories that may be removed periodically to frighten one's grandchildren to provide accompaniment to Spanish music.

DNA: A complex organic molecules characterized as the building block of life and death appropriately shaped like a Spiral staircase to nowhere.

Fiber: Edible wood-pulp said to aid digestion and prolong life, so that we might enjoy another six or o eight years in which to consume wood-pulp.

Genetic engineering: Tampering with chromosomes so that science might develop a new miracle cure or a rabbit that plays the banjo.

Math anxiety: An intense lifelong fear of two trains approaching each other at speeds of 60 and 80 miles an hour.

Neurotic: Sane but unhappy about it.

Obituary: A final summation of our lives that, for most of us, occupies about 3 inches of space that what we will shortly become cage liner for your neighbor's parakeet.

Positive thinking: Self-improvement through self-deception.

Quality of life: What an industrialized nation is said to offer when enough of its citizens are suffering from terminal Stress.

Urinal: The one place where all men are peers.

X-chromosome: A genetic double-cross that empowers women with the ability to bear children and reserves for men the right to be color blind hemophiliacs.

Zombie: A mirthless creature beloved by teenage horror movie fans and those in charge of the hiring and accounting firms.

THE TOP REJECTED NAMES FOR ANTI-IMPOTENCE DRUGS

Menicillin
Schwanzenhance
Wood 'n' Plenty
Chubbie Delight
BoneRite
Penochio
Presidentia
PharmaFluffer
Schwingicin-D
Wang Shui
Limpbengone

THE TOP NAMES PICKED FOR ANTI-IMPOTENCE DRUGS

Engorgia
Holyshitaril
Coxgro

Shaftlock
Slipitinur
The Bone-r
The Stiffer Pecker Upper
Blueveinertin
Chlortrioxide Benzoylacetate Tetraseptic Cock Strenghthener
Grecian Formula 6"
Kumincider
Pep to Jismol

GENETICS OF VAN GOGH'S RELATIVES

After much careful research, it has been discovered that the artist Vincent Van Gogh had many relatives. Among them were:
His dizzy aunt. Verti Gogh.
The brother who ate prunes. Gotta Gogh.
The brother who worked at a convenience store. Stopn Gogh.
The grandfather from Yugoslavia. U Gogh.
The brother who bleached his clothes white. Hue Gogh.
The cousin from Illinois. Chica Gogh.
His magician uncle. Wherediddy Gogh.
His Mexican cousin. Amee Gogh.
The Mexican cousin's American half brother. Grin Gogh.
The nephew who drove a stage coach. Wellsfar Gogh.
The constipated uncle. Cant Gogh.
The ballroom dancing aunt. Tan Gogh.
The bird lover uncle. Flamin Gogh.
His nephew psychoanalyst. E Gogh.
The fruit loving cousin . Man Gogh.
An aunt who taught positive thinking. Wayto Gogh.
The little bouncy nephew. Poe Gogh.
A sister who loved disco. Go Gogh.
His Italian uncle. Day Gogh.

And his niece who travels the country in a van. Winnie Bay Gogh.

THE PRESCRIPTION

A nice, calm and respectable lady went to the pharmacy, walked up to the pharmacist, looked straight into his eyes, and said, "I would like to buy some cyanide."

The pharmacist asked, "Why in the world do you need cyanide?"

The lady replied, "I need to poison my husband."

The pharmacist eyes got big and he exclaimed, "Lord have Mercy! I can't give you cyanide to kill your husband. That's against the law! I'll lose my license! They'll throw both of us in jail! All kinds of bad things will happen. Absolutely not! You cannot have any cyanide!" The lady reached into her purse and pulled out a picture of her husband in bed with the pharmacist wife. The pharmacist looked at the picture in replied, "Well now, that's different. You didn't tell me you had a prescription."

SCIENTIFIC ONE LINERS

Two antennas meet on a roof, fall in love and get married. The ceremony wasn't much, but the reception was excellent.

Two hydrogen atoms walk into a bar. One says, "I've lost my electron." The other says,

"Are you sure?" The first replies, "yes I'm positive."

A jumper cable walks into a bar. The bartender says, "I'll serve you but don't start anything."

"Doc, I can't stop singing "The Green, Green Grass of home." "That sounds like Tom Jones Syndrome." " Is it common?" Doc says,, "It's Not Unusual."

An invisible man marries an invisible woman. The kids were nothing to look at either.

CHAPTER 5 ANIMAL

THE BIRDS

Two vultures board an airplane, each carrying two dead racoons. The stewardess looks at them and says, "I'm sorry, gentlemen, only one carrion per passenger."

BOLL WEEVILS

Two boll weevils grew up in South Carolina. One went to Hollywood and became a famous actor. The other stayed behind in cotton fields and never amounted to much. The second one, naturally became known as the lesser of two weevils.

CAT HEAVEN

Clovis the cat died and went to heaven. God met her at the golden gate and said, "You have been a good cat all of these years. Anything you want is yours for the asking." Clovis thought a minute and then said, "All my life I've lived on a farm and slept on hard wooden floors. I'd like a real fluffy pillow to sleep on."

God said, "Say no more." Instantly Clovis had a huge fluffy pillow. A few days later, six mice were killed in an accident and they all went to heaven at the same time. God met the mice at the gates of heaven with the same offer that he had made to the cat. The mice said, "Well, we've had to run all of our lives from cats, dogs and even people with brooms. If we could just have some little roller skates, we'd never have to run again." God answered, It is done." And immediately the mice received beautiful little roller skates.

About a week later God decided to check on Clovis. He found her sound asleep on her fluffy pillow. God gently awakened her and asked, "Is every thing OK? How have you been doing? Are you happy?"Clovis replied, "Oh, it's wonderful. I've never been so happy in my life. My pillow is so fluffy, and those little meals on wheels you've been sending over are delicious!"

DOCTOR'S OPINION

A woman brought a very limp duck into a veterinary surgeon. As she lay her pet on the table, the vet pulled out his stethoscope and listened to the bird's chest. After a moment or two, the vet shook his head sadly and said, "I'm so sorry, your pet has passed away." The distressed owner wailed, "Are you sure? "Yes, I'm sure. The duck is dead," he replied. "How can you be so sure", she protested. "I mean, you haven't done any testing on him or anything. He might just be in a coma or something." The vet rolled his eyes, turned around and left the room. He returned a few moments later with a black Labrador retriever. As the duck's owner looked on in amazement, the dog stood on his hind legs, put his front paws on the examination table and sniffed the duck from top to bottom. He then looked at the vet with sad eyes and shook his head. The vet patted the dog and took it out and returned a few moments later with a beautiful cat. The cat jumped up on the table and also sniffed the bird from its beak to its tail and back again. The cat sat back on its haunches, shook its head, meowed softly, jumped down and strolled out of the room. The vet looked at the woman and said, "I'm sorry, but as I said, this is most definitely, 100% certifiably, a dead duck." Then the vet turned to his computer terminal, hit a few keys and produced a bill, which he handed to the woman. The duck's owner, still in shock, took the bill. "$150!" she cried."$150 just to tell me my duck is dead?!!" The vet shrugged. "I'm sorry. If you'd taken my word for it, the bill would have been $20.But what with the Lab Report and the Cat Scan, it all adds up."

GRIZZLY BEAR

A hawk, a lion and a skunk argued heatedly about who was the most important animal in the forest. They made so much noise that they didn't hear the grizzly bear sneaking up. He swallowed them all, hawk, lion and stinker!

CAT AND MOUSE

Clovis the cat died and went to heaven. God met her at the golden gate and said, "You have been a good cat all of these years. Anything you want is yours for the asking."

Clovis thought a minute and then said, "All my life I've lived on a farm and slept on Hardwood floors. I'd like a real fluffy pillow to sleep on."

God said, "Say no more."Instantly Clovis had a huge fluffy pillow.

A few days later, six mice were killed in an accident and they all went to heaven.

At the same time. God met the mice at the gates of heaven with the same offer that he had made to the cat. The mice said, "Well we've had to run all of our lives from cats, dogs, and even people with brooms. If we could just have some little roller skates, we'd never have to run again."

God answered, "It is done." And immediately the mice received beautiful little roller skates.

About a week later God decided to check on Clovis. He found her sound asleep on her fluffy pillow. God gently awakened her and asked, "Is everything OK? How have you been doing? Are you happy?"

Clovis replied, "Oh, it's wonderful. I've never been so happy in my life. My pillow is so

fluffy, and those little meals on wheels you've been sending over are delicious!"

CAMEL SEX

A new Marine Captain was assigned to an outfit in a remote post in the Afghanistan Desert. During his first inspection of the outfit, he noticed a Camel hitched up behind the mess tent.

He asks the Sergeant why the camel is kept there. The nervous sergeant said, "Well sir, as you know, there are 250 men here on the post and no women. And sir, sometimes the men have "urges".

That's why we have Molly The Camel." The Captain says, "I can't say that I condone this, but I understand about "urges", so the camel can stay ."

About a month later, the Captain starts having his own "urges". Crazy with passion, he asks the Sergeant to bring the camel to his tent. Putting a ladder behind the camel, the Captain stands on the ladder, pulls his pants down and has wild, insane sex with the camel. When he's done, he asks the Sergeant, "Is that how the men do it?" "No not really, sir..They usually just ride the camel into town where the girls are."!

MOLES

A mama mole, a papa mole, and a baby mole all live in a little mole hole.

One day the papa moe sticks his head out of the hole, sniffs the air and says, "Yum! I smell maple syrup!." The mama mole sticks her head out of the hole, sniffs the air and says "Yum! I smell honey!"

The baby mole tries to stick his head out of the hole to sniff the air, but can't

Because the bigger moles are in the way so he says, "Geez, all I can smell is molasses."

ZOO

What 's the difference between a Southern Zoo and a Northern Zoo?

A Southern Zoo has a description of the animal on the front of the cage, along with a recipe.

RABBIT

How do you catch a unique rabbit? Unique up on it.

How do you catch a tame rabbit? Tame Way, unique up on it.

FISH

What do fish say when they hit a concrete wall? Dam!

COW

What do you get from a pampered cow? Spoiled milk.

DOG

Where do you find a dog with no legs? Where you left him.

GORILLAS

Why do gorillas have big nostrils? Because they have big fingers.

SNAIL

A snail grew tired of his reputation for being slow. He decided to getsome fast wheels--a Nissan 350Z. But he insisted that it be changed to a 350S. "S stands for snail," he said. "I want everybody who sees me roaring past to know who's driving." The dealer complied. Pretty soon, the snail was roaring down the highway. And when people saw him zooming by, they'd say, "Wow! Look at that S-car go!"

ROOSTER

A farmer goes out one day and buys a brand new stud rooster to copulate with his chickens. The farmer puts the rooster straight in the pen so he can get down to business.

The young rooster walks over to the old rooster and says "Ok, old fellow, time to retire."

The old rooster says, "you can't handle all these chickens.. look at what it did to me!"

The young rooster replies, "Now, don't give me a hassle about this. Time for the old to step aside and the young to take over, so take a hike." The old rooster says, "Aw, c'mon... just let me have the two old hens over in the corner. I won't bother you," The young rooster says, "Scram! Beat it! You're washed up!!! I'm taking over!"

So, the old rooster thinks for a minute and then says to the young rooster, "I'll tell you what, young fellow, I'll have a race with you around the farmhouse. Whoever wins the race gets domain of the chicken coop. And if I'm so feeble, why not give me a little head start?"

The young rooster says, 'Sure, why not, you know I'll still beat you." They go to the henhouse and get in position. "Go!" and the old rooster takes off running. About 15 seconds later the young rooster takes off after him. They round the front of the farmhouse and the young rooster is only about 5 inches behind the old rooster and gaining fast. The farmer, sitting on the porch, looks up, sees what's going on, grabs his shotgun and BOOM!, he blows the young rooster to fried chicken heaven. He shakes his head gloomily and says "Son of a gun…third gay rooster I bought this week!"

WHY DID THE CHICKEN CROSS THE ROAD?

Vice President Gore

I fight for the chickens and I am fighting for the chickens right now.

I will not give up on the chickens crossing the road! I will fight for the chickens and I will not disappoint them.

Governor George W. Bush

I don't believe we need to get the chickens across the road. I say give the road to the chickens and let them decide. The government needs to let go of strangling the chickens so they can get across the road.

Senator Lieberman

I believe that every chicken has the right to worship their God in their own way. Crossing the road is a spiritual journey and no chicken should be denied the right to cross the road in their own way.

Secretary Cheney
Chickens are big-time because they have wings. They could fly if they wanted to. Chickens don't want to cross the road. They don't need help crossing the road. In fact, I'm not interested in crossing the road myself.

Ralph Nader
Chickens are misled into believing there is a road by the evil tire makers. Chickens aren't ignorant, but our society pays tire makers to create the need for these roads and then lures chickens into believing there is an advantage to crossing them. Down with the roads, up with chickens.

Pat Buchanan
To steal a job from a decent, hardworking American.

Jerry Falwell
Because the chicken was gay! Isn't it obvious? Can't you people see the plain truth in front of your face? The chicken was going to the "other side." That's what "they" call it –the "other side." Yes, my friends, that chicken is gay. And, if you eat that chicken, you will become gay too. I say we boycott all chickens until we sort out this abomination that the liberal media whitewashes with seemingly harmless phrases like "the other side." That chicken should not be free to cross the road. It's as plain and simple as that.

Dr. Seuss
Did the chicken cross the road?
Did he cross it with a toad?
Yes! The chicken crossed the road, but why it crossed, I've not been told!

Ernest Hemingway
To die, In the rain.

Martin Luther King, Jr.
I envisioned a world where all chickens will be free to cross without having their motives called into question.

GrandPa
In my day, we didn't ask why the chicken crossed the road. Someone told us that the chicken crossed the road, and that was good enough for us.

Aristotle
It is the nature of chickens to cross the road

Karl Marx
It was a historical inevitability

Saddam Hussein
This was an unprovoked act of rebellion and we were quite justified in dropping nerve gas on it.

Captain James T. Kirk
To boldly go where no chicken has gone before.

Fox Mulder
You saw it cross the road with your own eyes. How many more chickens have to cross before you believe it?

Freud
The fact that you are all concerned that the chicken crossed the road reveals your underlying sexual insecurity.

Bill Gates
I have just released eChicken 2000, which will not only cross roads, but will lay eggs, file your important documents, and balance your checkbook.

Einstien
Did the chicken really cross the road, or did the road move beneath the chicken?

Bill Clinton
I did not cross the road with THAT chicken. What do you mean by "Chicken"?
Could you define "chicken" please?

Louis Farrakhan
The road, you will see, represents the black man. The chicken crossed the "black man" in order to trample him and keep him down.

Colonel Sanders
I missed one?

Barack Obama
Tell the people that the chicken crossed the road, when he didn't, and make them believe it.
The moral of the story is too many chickens had crossed the road leading to overcrowding and they met Sam and Ella.

ELEPHANT

Where do you find elephants? That depends where you lost them.

Why do elephants wear blue tennis shoes? Because white ones get dirty too fast.

Why do elephants live in herds? To get wholesale reduction on blue tennis shoes.

Why do elephants float on their backs? So they don't get their tennis shoes wet.

How many elephants can you fit in a taxi? Four (one next to the driver and three in the back).

How many giraffes can you fit in a taxi? None, it's already full of elephants.

What sport do elephants play in a taxi? Squash.

How do you know when an elephant is visiting your house? There's a taxi outside with three elephants in it.

How do you put an elephant into the refrigerator? Open door, put elephant in, close door.

How do you put a giraffe into a refrigerator? Open door, get elephant out, put giraffe in, close door.

How can you tell when there's been an elephant in your refrigerator? Footprints in the butter.

How can you tell there is an elephant in your refrigerator? Blue tennis shoes are left outside.

How can you tell where there are two elephants in your refrigerator? It's rather hard to close the door.

How can you tell when there've been four elephants in your refrigerator? There's a taxi waiting outside.

ROSWELL

You may remember that on July 8, 1947, witnesses claim a spaceship with five aliens aboard crashed on a sheep and cattle ranch outside Roswell, N.M. This is an incident, of course, that Many say has been covered up by the government. However, you may not know that on March 31, 1948, exactly nine months after that day, Al Gore was born. Now that clears up a lot of things.

ANIMAL ONE LINERS

Two cows standing next to each other in a field, Daisy says to Dolly, "I was artificially inseminated this morning." "I don't believe you," said dolly. "It's true, no bull!" Exclaimed Daisy.

DOG EYES

A man takes his Rottweiler to the vet and says, "My dog's cross eyed, is there anything you can do for him?" "Well, " says the vet, "let's have a look at him." So he picks the dog up and examines the eyes, then checks his teeth. Finally, he says, " I'm going to have to put him down."

"What? Because he's cross eyed?" "No, because he's really heavy."

CHAPTER 6 BLONDE, BRUNETTE, REDHEAD

THE COMPACT

Two blondes are walking down the street. One notices a compact on the sidewalk and leans down to pick it up. She opens it, looks in the mirror and says, "Hmm, this person looks familiar." The second blonde says, "Here, let me see!" So the first blonde hands her the compact. The second one looks in the mirror and says, "You dummy, it's me!

EXPOSURE

A blonde is walking down the street with her blouse open and her right breast hanging out. A policeman approaches her and says,

"Ma'am, are you aware that I could cite you for indecent exposure?"

She says, "Why, officer?" "Because your breast is hanging out." he says.

She looks down and says, "OH MY GOD, I left the baby on the bus again!"

KNITTING

A highway patrolman pulled alongside a speeding car on the freeway. Glancing at the car, he was astounded to see that the blonde behind the wheel was knitting! Realizing that she was oblivious to his flashing lights and siren, the trooper cranked down his window, turned on his bullhorn and yelled, "PULL OVER!" "NO!" the blonde yelled back, "IT'S A SCARF!"

IN A VACUUM

A blonde was playing Trivial Pursuit one night. It was her turn. She rolled the dice and she landed on Science & Nature. Her question was, "If you are in a vacuum and someone calls your name, can you hear it?"She thought for a time and then asked, "Is it on or off?"

RIVER WALK

There's this blonde out for a walk. She comes to a river and sees another blonde on the opposite bank. Yoo-hoo!" she shouts, "How can I get to the other side?" The second blonde looks up the river then down the river and shouts back , "You ARE on the other side."

FLIGHT

A blonde calls Delta Airlines and asks, "Can you tell me how long it'll take to fly from San Francisco to New York City?"

The agent replies, "Just a minute..." "Thank you," the blonde says, and hangs up.

CURIOSITY

This guy has been sitting in a bar all night, staring at a blonde wearing, the tightest pants he's ever seen. Finally his curiosity gets the best of him, so he walks over and asks, "How do you get into those pants?"

The young woman looks him over and replies, "Well, you could start by buying me a drink."

ENERGY EFFICIENT

Last year I replaced all the windows in my house with those expensive double-pane energy efficient kind....But this week I got a call from the contractor complaining that his work had been completed a whole year ago and I had yet to pay for them. Boy oh boy, did we go around!! Just because I'm blonde doesn't mean that I am automatically stupid...So, I proceeded to tell him just what his fast talking sales guy had told me last year...that in one year the windows would pay for themselves. There was silence on the other end of the line, so I just hung up and I have not heard back.

THE FIRST BLONDE MALE JOKE

The Sheriff in a small town walks out in the street and sees a blond cowboy coming down the walk with nothing on but his cowboy hat, gun and his boots, so he arrests him for indecent exposure. As he is locking him up, he asks "Why in the world are you dressed like this?" The Cowboy says "Well it's like this Sheriff... I was in the bar down the road and this pretty little red head asks me to go out to her motor home with her... so I did. We go inside and she pulls off her top and asks me to pull off my shirt.. so I did. Then she pulls off her skirt and asks me to pull off my pants... so I did Then she pulls off her panties and asks me to pull off my shorts... so I did. Then she gets on the bed and looks at me kind of sexy and says, "Now go to town cowboy... " And here I am.

BLONDE LOOKING FOR SHOES

Alligator shoes for a   blonde. A young blonde was on vacation in the depths of Louisiana. She wanted a pair of genuine alligator shoes in the worst way, but was very reluctant to pay the high prices the local vendors were asking. After becoming very frustrated with the "no haggle" attitude of one of the shopkeepers, the blonde shouted, "Maybe I'll just go out and catch my own alligator so I can get a pair of shoes at a reasonable price!" The shopkeeper said "By all means, be my guest. Maybe you'll luck out and catch yourself a big one!" Determined, the blonde turned and headed for the swamps, set on catching herself an alligator. Later in the day, the shopkeeper is driving home, when he spots the young woman standing waist deep in the water, shotgun in hand. Just then, he sees a huge 9 foot alligator swimming quickly toward her. She takes aim, kills the creature and with a great deal of effort hauls it on to the swamp bank. Laying nearby were several more of the dead creatures. The shopkeeper watched in amazement. Just then the blonde flips the alligator on it's back, and frustrated, shouts out, "Damn! This one is barefoot, too!"

COAST

A married couple was asleep when the phone rang at 2 in the morning. The wife (undoubtedly blonde), picked up the phone, listened a moment and said, "How should I know, that's 200 miles from here!" and hung up. The husband said, "Who was that?" The wife said, "I don't know, some woman wanting to know if the coast is clear."

THE BLONDE AND THE GUN

A blonde suspects her boyfriend of cheating on her, so she goes out and buys a gun. She goes to his apartment unexpectedly and when she opens the door she finds him in the arms of a redhead. Well, the blonde is really angry. She opens her purse to take out the gun, and as she does so, she is overcome with grief.

She takes the gun and puts it to her head. The boyfriend yells, "No, honey, don't do it!!!" The blonde replies, "Shut up, you're next!"

THE QUESTION
What did the blonde ask her doctor when he told her she was pregnant? "Is it mine?"

ROE VS. WADE
Bambi, a blonde in her fourth year as a UCLA freshman, sat in her US government class. The professor asked Bambi if she knew what Roe vs.

Wade was about. Bambi pondered the question then finally said, "That was the decision George Washington had to make before he crossed the Delaware"

THE ELECTRIC CHAIR
Three women go down to Mexico one night, get drunk, and wake up in jail, only to find that they are to be executed in he morning, though none of them can remember what they did the night before.

The first one, a redhead, is strapped in the electric chair, and is asked if she has any last words. She says, "I am from Grace University, and believe in the almighty power of God to intervene on the behalf of the innocent," They throw the switch and nothing happens. They all immediately prostrate themselves; beg for her forgiveness, and release her. The second one, a brunette, is strapped in and gives her last words, "I am from the Creighton Schoolof Law and I believe in the power of justice to intervene on the part of the innocent." They throw the switch and again, nothing happens.Again, they all immediately prostrate themselves; beg for her forgiveness, and release her.

The last one, a blond, is strapped in and says, "Well, I'm from the University of Iowa, Iowa City and just graduated with a degree in Electrical Engineering, and I'll tell you right now, you ain't gonna electrocute nobody if you don't plug this thing in."

THE TWO BLONDES

Two blondes living in Oklahoma were sitting on a bench one evening, looking at the moon and talking.

One blonde says to the other, "Which do you think is farther .... Florida or the moon"?

The other blonde rolls her eyes, turns and says, "Hellooooooooooooooooooooo, can you see Florida from here?"...

BLONDE AND A ROOFER

A Blonde and a Roofer are on the phone discussing meeting at Menardes to buy a door for an apartment. The Roofer says I will meet you in the parking lot in 25 minutes. The blonde askes where in the parking lot?

The roofer says in between the blue lines on the asphalt.

STATE CAPITALS

A blonde was bragging about her knowledge of state capitols. She proudly says, "Go ahead, ask me, I know all of them."

A friend says, "OK, what's the capitol of Wisconsin?"

The blonde replies, "Oh, that's easy: **W**."

SNOWY DAY

Norman and his wife live in Calgary. One winter morning while listening to the Radio, they hear the announcer say "We are going to have 8 to 10 centimeters of snow today. You must park your car on the even numbered side of the street so the snow plowcan get through."

Norman's wife goes out and moves her car. A week later while they are eating Breakfast, the radio announcer says "We are expecting 10 to 12 centimeters of snow today. You must park on the odd side of the street so the snow plow can Get through."

Norman's wife moves the car again. The next week the announcer says on the radio "We are expecting 12 to 14 centimeters of snow. You must park.... " then the electric power goes out.

Norman's wife is very upset, and with a worried look on her face says, "Honey, I don't know what to do . which side of the street do I need to park this time.

With Love and understanding in his voice like all of us men married to blondes exhibit, Norman says, "Why don't you just leave it in the garage this time.?"

REDHEAD JOKE

A gorgeous young redhead goes into the doctor's office and says that her body hurts wherever she touches it. "Impossible!" says the doctor. "Show me." The redhead takes her finger, pushes on her left breast and screams, then she pushes her elbow and screams in even more agony. She pushes her knee and screams; likewise she pushes her ankle and screams. Everywhere she touches makes her scream. The doctor says, "You're not really a redhead, are you? "Well, no" she says, "I'm actually a blonde." "I thought so," the doctor says. "Your finger is broken."

DOG

Two blondes are walking down the road when one says, Look at that dog with one eye!

The other blonde covers one of her eyes and says, Where?

ICE FISHING

A blonde decided she needed something new and different for a winter hobby.

She went to the bookstore and bought every book she could find on ice fishing.

For weeks she read and studied, hoping to become an expert in the field.

Finally she decided she knew enough, and out she went for her first ice fishing trip.

She carefully gathered up and packed all the tools and equipment needed for the excursion.

Each piece of equipment had its own special place in her kit. When she got to the ice, she found a quiet little area, placed her padded stool, and carefully laid out her tools. Just as she was about to make her first cut into the ice, a booming voice from the sky bellowed, "There are no fish under the ice!"

Startled, the blonde grabbed up all her belongings, moved further along the ice, poured some hot chocolate from her thermos, and started to cut a new hole. Again the voice from above bellowed, "there are no fish under the ice!" Amazed, the blonde wasn't quite sure what to do, as this certainly wasn't covered in any of her books. She packed up her gear and moved to the far side of the ice. Once there, she stopped for a few moments to regain her calm. Then she was extremely careful to set everything up perfectly her tools in the right place, chair positioned just so. Just as she was about to cut this new hole, the voice came again, "There are no fish under the ice!"

Petrified, the blonde looked skyward and asked: "Is that you Lord?"

The voiced boomed back, "No, this is the manager of the skating rink!"

PLANE RIDE

A plane is on its way to Montreal when a blonde in Economy class gets up and moves to the First Class section and sits down. The flight attendant watches her do this and asks to see her ticket. She then tells the blonde that she paid for Economy and that she will have to sit in the back.

The blonde replies "I'm blonde, I'm beautiful, I'm going to Montreal and I'm staying right here!"

The flight attendant goes into the cockpit and tells the pilot and co-pilot that there is some blonde bimbo sitting in First Class that belongs in Economy and won't move back to her seat.

The blonde replies, "I'm blonde, I'm beautiful, I'm going to Montreal and I'm staying right here!"

The co-pilot goes back to the blonde and tries to explain that because she is only paid for Economy she will have to leave and return to her seat.

The blonde replies, "I'm blonde, I'm beautiful, I'm going to Montreal and I'm staying right here!"

The co-pilot tells the pilot that he probably should have the police waiting when they land to arrest this Blonde woman that won't listen to reason.

The pilot says "You say she's blonde? I'll handle this. I'm married to a blonde. I speak 'blonde'!"

He goes back to the blonde, whispers in her ear, and she says "Oh, I'm sorry" gets up and moves back to her seat in the Economy section.

The flight attendant and co-pilot are amazed and asked him what he said to make her move without any fuss. "I told her First Class isn't going to Montreal."

SCHOOL

A brunette, a blonde, and a redhead are all in third grade. Who has the biggest boobs? The blonde because she's 18.

RULE

What do you call a brilliant blonde?
A Golden retriever.

AIRLINE FLIGHT

A blonde and a lawyer are seated next to each other on a flight from Los Angeles to New York.

The lawyer asks if she would like to play a fun game. The blonde, tired, just wants to take a nap, so she politely declines and rolls over to the window to catch a few winks. The lawyer persists and explains that the game is easy and lot of fun. He says, "I ask you a question, and if you don't know the answer, you pay me $5, and vice versa."

Again, she declines and tries to get some sleep.

The lawyer, now agitated, says, "Okay, if you don't know the answer, you pay me $5, and if I don't know the answer, I will pay you $500. This catches the blonde's attention and , figuring there will be no end to this torment, agrees to the game.

The lawyer asks the first question: "What's the distance from the earth to the moon?" The blonde doesn't say a word, reaches into her purse, pulls out a $5 bill, and hands it to the lawyer.

"Okay, says the lawyer, "your turn."

She asks, "What goes up a hill with three legs and comes down with four legs?"

The lawyer, puzzled, takes out his laptop computer and searches all his references.. no answer. He taps into the air phone with his modem and searches the Internet and the Library of Congress.. no answer.

Frustrated, he sends e-mails to all his friends and coworkers but to no avail.

After an hour, he wakes the blonde and hands her $500. The blonde thanks him and turns back to get some sleep. The lawyer, who is more than miffed, stirs the blonde and asks, "Well, what's the answer?"

Without a word, the blonde reaches into her purse, hands the lawyer $5, and goes back to sleep.

VENTRILOQUIST

A young ventriloquist is touring the clubs and one night he's doing a show in a small town in Kentucky

With his dummy on his knee, he's going through his usual dumb blonde jokes.

Suddenly, a blonde woman in the 4th row stands on her chair and starts shouting. "I've heard enough of your stupid blonde jokes. What makes you think you can stereotype woman that way? What does the color of a person's hair have to do with her worth as a human being? It's guys like you who keep women like me form being respected at work and tin the community and from reaching their full potential as a person, because you and your kind continue to perpetuate discrimination against no only blondes, but women in general. And all in the name of humor!" The embarrassed ventriloquist begins to apologize, when the blonde yells, "You stay out of this, mister! I'm talking to that little bastard on your knee!"

FIRST AID

"How come you're late?" asked the bartender, as the blonde waitress walked into the bar.

"It was a terrible accident. A man was thrown from his car and he was lying in the middle of the street. Hi leg was broken, his skull was fractured, and there was blood everywhere. Thank god I took that first-aid Course. "What did you do?" asked the bartender.

"I sat down and put my head between my knees to keep from fainting!"

COSMETIC SURGERY

Two women were having lunch together, and discussing the merits of cosmetic surgery. The first woman says, "Ineed to be honest with you, I'm getting a boob job. The second woman says "Oh that's nothing, I'm having my asshole bleached!" To which the first replies, "Whoa I just can't picture your husband as a blonde.!"

REDHEADS

How do you get a redhead to argue with you? Say something.

How do you get a redhead's mood to change? Wait 10 seconds.

If you love a redhead, set her free. If she follows you everywhere you go, pitches a tent in your front lawn and puts your new girlfriend in the hospital, she's yours.

What's safer, a redhead or a piranha? The piranha. They only attack in schools.

How do you know a guy at the beach has a redhead for a girlfriend? She has scratched "stay off MY TURF!" on his back with her nails.

What do you call a redhead with an attitude? Normal.

What does a redhead, an anniversary, and a toilet have in common? Men always miss them.

What do you call a woman who knows where her husband is every night? A redhead.

How do you know when your redhead has forgiven you? She stops washing your clothes in the toilet bowl.

How do you know when a redhead has been using your computer? There's a hammer in your monitor.

Only two things are necessary to keep a redhead happy. One is to let her think she is having her own way and the other is to let her have it.

How do you know when you haven't learned anything? When your school teacher is a redhead.

BRUNETTES

What's black and blue and brown and laying in a ditch? A brunette who's told too many blonde jokes.

What do you call going on a blind date with a brunette? Brown-bagging it.

What's the real reason a brunette keeps her figure? No one else wants it.

Why are so many blonde jokes one-liners? So brunettes can remember them.

What do you call a brunette in a room full of blondes? Invisible.

What's a brunette's mating call? "Has the blonde left yet?"

Why didn't Indians scalp brunettes? The hair from a buffalo's hump is more manageable.

Why is a brunette considered an evil color? When was the last time you saw a blonde witch.

What do brunettes miss most about a great party? The invitation.

What do you call a good looking man with a brunette? A hostage.

Who makes bras for brunettes? Fisher-Price.

Why are brunettes so proud of their hair? It matches their mustache.

BLONDE ONE LINER

Why are all dumb blonde jokes one liners? So men can understand them.

What did the blonde say when she saw the sign in front of the YMCA? "Look!" They spelled MACY'S wrong.

What is the definition of eternity? 4 blondes at a 4-way stop.

What do you call five blondes at the bottom of the ocean? An air pocket.

What do you call a basement full of blondes? A whine cellar.

BLONDE SPRAY CAN

A man was driving along the highway and saw a rabbit hopping across the middle of the road. He swerved to avoid hitting it, but unfortunately the hare jumped in front of the car and was hit. The driver, being a sensitive man as well as an animal lover, pulled over to the side of the road and got out to see what had become of the rabbit. Much to his dismay, the little animal was dead. The driver felt so awful he began to cry. A blonde woman driving down the highway saw the man crying on the side of the road and pulled over .She stepped out of her car and asked the man what was wrong. "I feel just terrible," he explained.

"I accidentally hit this little bunny, and I killed it." The woman told the man not to worry; she knew what to do. She went to her car, opened the door, reached into a bag inside, and pulled out a spray can . She walked over to the limp, dead rabbit and sprayed the contents of the can onto its lifeless form. Miraculously, the rabbit came to life! It jumped up, waved a forepaw at the two humans, turned, and hopped down the road. Ten feet away the rabbit stopped, turned around, waved at the two people again, then resumed hopping. Every ten feet or so, it turned and seemed to wave, then began hopping again. This kept on until the rabbit was out of sight. The last the man saw of it, it was still waving its front paw at him. The man was astonished! He couldn't figure out what had happened, or what substance could be in the woman's spray can. He ran over to the woman and demanded, "What was in the can? What did you put on that rabbit?" The woman turned the can around so he could read the label. It read, "Hair Spray.

Restores Life to Dead Hair. Adds Permanent Wave."

EXAMINATION DAY

The blonde reported for her university final exam which consists of "yes/no" type questions. She takes her seat in the examination hall, stares at the question and paper for five minutes, and then in a fit of inspiration takes her purse out, removes a coin and starts tossing the coin and marking the answers sheet.

Yes for heads, and no for tails. Within half an hour she is all done whereas the rest of the class is sweating it out. During the last few minutes, she is seen desperately throwing a coin, muttering in sweating. The moderator, alarmed, approaches her and asks what is going on? " I finished the exam in a half an hour, but I'm re- checking my answers.

CHAPTER 7 MEN

THE STORY OF MY LIFE ...

When I was 14, I hoped that one day I would have a girlfriend. When I was 16, I got a girlfriend, but there was no passion, so I decided I needed a passionate girl with a zest for life. In college I dated a passionate girl, but she was too emotional. Everything was an emergency; she was a drama queen, cried all the time and threatened suicide. So I decided I needed a girl with stability. When I was 25, I found a very stable girl but she was boring. She was totally predictable and never got excited about anything. Life became so dull that I decided that I needed a girl with some excitement. When I was 28, I found an exciting girl, but I couldn't keep up with her. She rushed from one thing to another, never settling on anything. She did mad impetuous things and made me miserable as often as happy. She was great fun initially and very energetic, but directionless. So I decided to find a girl with some real ambition. When I turned 31, I found a smart ambitious girl with her feet planted firmly on the ground and married her. She was so ambitious that she divorced me and took everything I owned. I am now older and wiser, and am looking for a girl with big tits.

CONDOMS

Why Condoms Come in Boxes of 3, 6, or 12 A man walks into a drug store with his 8-year-old son. They happen to walk by the condom display, and the boy asks, "What are these, Dad?" The man matter-of-factly replies, "Those are called condoms, son. Men use them to have safe sex." "Oh, I see," replied the boys pensively. "Yes, I've heard of that in health class at school." He looks over the display, picks up a package of three condoms and asks, "Why are there three in this package?" The dad replies, "Those are for high school boys: one for Friday, one for Saturday, and one for Sunday." "Cool!" says the boy. He notices a 6-pack and asks, "Then who are these for?" "Those are for college men," the dad answers. "TWO for Friday, TWO for Saturday, and TWO for Sunday." "! WOW!" exclaims the boy. "Then who uses THESE?" he asks, picking up a 12-pack. With a sigh, the dad replies, "Those are for married men. One for January, one for February, one for March........"

CALLING IN SICK

Calling in sick to work makes me uncomfortable. No matter how legitimate my excuse, I always get the feeling that my boss thinks I'm lying. On one recent occasion, I had a valid reason but lied anyway, because the truth was just too darned humiliating. I simply mentioned that I had sustained a head injury, and I hoped I would feel up to coming in the next day. By then, I reasoned, I could think up a doozy to explain the bandage on the top of my head. The accident occurred mainly because I had given in to my wife's wishes to adopt a cute little kitty. Initially, the new acquisition was no problem. Then one morning, I was taking my shower after breakfast when I heard my wife, Deb, call out to me from the kitchen. "Honey ! The garbage disposal is dead again. Please come reset it." "You know where the button is," I protested through the shower pitter-patter and steam. "Reset it yourself!" "But I'm scared!" she persisted. "What if it starts going and sucks me in?" There was a meaningful pause and then, "C'mon, it'll only take you a second." So out I came, dripping wet and buck naked, hoping that my silent outraged nudity would make a statement about how I perceived her behavior as extremely cowardly. Sighing loudly, I squatted down and stuck my head under the sink to find the button. It is the last action I remember performing. It struck without warning, and without any respect to my circumstances. No, it wasn't the hexed disposal, drawing me into its gnashing metal teeth. It was our new kitty, who discovered the fascinating dangling objects she spied hanging between my legs. She had been poised around the corner and stalked me as I reached under the sink. And, at the precise moment when I was most vulnerable, she leapt at the toys I unwittingly offered and snagged them with her needle-like claws. I lost all rational thought to control orderly bodily movements, blindly rising at a violent rate of speed, with the full weight of a kitten hanging from my masculine region. Wild animals are sometimes faced with a fight or flight syndrome. Men, in this predicament, choose only the "flight" option. I know this from experience. I was fleeing straight up into the air when the sink and cabinet bluntly and forcefully impeded my ascent. The impact knocked me out cold. When I awoke, my wife and the paramedics stood over me. Now there are not many things in this life worse than finding oneself lying on the kitchen floor buck naked in front of a group of "been-here, done-that" paramedics. Even worse, having been fully briefed by my wife, the paramedics were all snorting loudly as they tried to conduct their work, all the while trying to suppress their hysterical laughter... and not succeeding. Somehow I lived through it all. A few days later I finally made it back in to the office, where colleagues tried to coax an explanation out of me about my head injury. I kept silent, claiming it was too painful to talk about. Which it was. "What's the matter?" They all asked, "Cat got your tongue?"

MEN, WHO UNDERSTANDS THEM?

The nice men are ugly.

The handsome men are not nice.

The handsome and nice men are gay.

The handsome, nice, and heterosexual men are married.

The men who are not so handsome, but are nice men, have no money.

The men who are not so handsome, but are nice men with money, think we are only after their money.

The handsome men without money are after our money.

The handsome men who are not so nice and somewhat heterosexual, don't think we are beautiful enough.

The men who think we are beautiful, that are heterosexual, somewhat nice, and have money are cowards.

The men who are somewhat handsome, somewhat nice, have some money, and thank God, are heterosexual, are shy and never make the first move! The men who never make the first move, automatically lose interest in us when we take the initiative.

NOW, WHO THE HELL UNDERSTANDS MEN??

ABBOT AND COSTELLO AT EXTRA SPECIAL COMPUTER STORE

ABBOTT (behind the computer at Extra Special computer store): Can I help you?

COSTELLO: Thanks. I'm setting up an office in my den, and I'm thinking about buying a computer.

ABBOTT: Mac?

COSTELLO: No, the name's Lou.

ABBOTT: Your computer?

COSTELLO: I don't own a computer. I want to buy one.

ABBOTT: Mac?

COSTELLO: I told you my name's Lou.

ABBOTT: What about Windows?

COSTELLO: Why? Will it get stuffy in here?

ABBOTT: Do you want a computer with Windows?

COSTELLO: I don't know. What will I see when I look in the windows?

ABBOTT: Wallpaper.

COSTELLO: Never mind the windows. I need a computer and software.

ABBOTT: Software for Windows?

COSTELLO: No. On the computer! I need something I can use to write proposals, track expenses and ran my business. What have you got?

ABBOTT: Office.

COSTELLO: Yeah, for my office. Can you recommend anything?

ABBOTT: I just did.

COSTELLO: You just did what?

ABBOTT: Recommend something.

COSTELLO: You recommended something?

ABBOTT: Yes.

COSTELLO: For my office?

ABBOTT: Yes.

COSTELLO: OK, what did you recommend for my office?

ABBOTT: Office.

COSTELLO: Yes, for my office!

ABBOTT: I recommended Office with Windows.

COSTELLO: I already have an office and it has windows! OK, lets just say, I'm setting at my computer and I want to type my proposal. What do I need?

ABBOTT: Word.

COSTELLO: What word?

ABBOTT: Word in Office.

COSTELLO: The only word in office is office.

ABBOTT: The Word in Office for Windows.

COSTELLO: Which word in office for windows?

ABBOTT: The Word you get when you click the blue "W"
continued next page

COSTELLO: I'm going to click your blue "W" if you don't
start withsome straight answers. OK, forget that. Can I watch
movies on the Internet?

ABBOTT: Yes, you want Real One.

COSTELLO: Maybe a real one, maybe a cartoon. What I
watch is none of your business. Just tell me what I need!

ABBOTT: Real One.

COSTELLO: If it's a long movie I also want to see reel 2,3
&4. Can I watch them?

ABBOTT: Of course.

COSTELLO: Great, with what?

ABBOTT: Real One.

COSTELLO: OK, I'm at my computer and I want to watch
a movie. What do I do?

ABBOTT: You click the blue "1"

COSTELLO: I click the blue one what?

ABBOTT: The blue "1"

COSTELLO: Is that different from the blue "W"?

ABBOTT: The blue "1" is Real One and the blue "W" is
Word.

COSTELLO: What word?

ABBOTT: The Word in Office for Windows.

COSTELLO: But there's three words in "office for windows!"

ABBOTT: No, just one. But it's the most popular Word in
the world.

COSTELLO: It is?

ABBOTT: Yes, but to be fair, there aren't many other Words
left. It pretty much wiped out all the other Words out there.

COSTELLO: And that word is real one?

ABBOTT: Real One has nothing to do with Word. Real One
isn't even part of Office.

COSTELLO: Stop! Don't start that again. What about financial bookkeeping, you have anything I can track my money with?

ABBOTT: Money.

COSTELLO: That's right. What do you have?

ABBOTT: Money.

COSTELLO: I need money to track my money?

ABBOTT: It comes bundled with your computer.

COSTELLO: What's bundled to my computer?

ABBOTT: Money.

COSTELLO: Money comes with my computer?

ABBOTT: Yes, No extra charge.

COSTELLO: I get a bundle of money with my computer. How much?

ABBOTT: One copy.

COSTELLO: Isn't it illegal to copy money?

ABBOTT: Microsoft gave us a license to copy Money.

COSTELLO: They can give you a license to copy money?

ABBOTT: Why not? THEY OWN IT!

COSTELLO: How do I turn my computer off?

ABBOTT: Click on "START"..........

BALDNESS

If a man is bald in the front he is a thinker.

If a man is bald in the back he is a lover.

If a man is bald in the front and back he thinks he is a lover.

CHEMISTRY LESSON

Element name: Manium

Symbol: XY

Atomic Weight :180 + or _ 50

Physical Properties: Solid at room temperature, but gets bent out of shape easily. It is

fairly dense and sometimes flaky. Also, difficult to find a pure sample. Due to rust, aging samples are unable to create electricity as easily as younger samples.

Chemical Properties: Attempts to bond with WO any chance it can get. Also tends to form strong bonds with itself. Becomes explosive when mixed with KD (Element: Childium) for prolonged

periods of time. Neutralize by saturating with alcohol.

Usage: None known. Possible good methane source. Good samples are able to produce large quantities on command.

Caution: In the absence of WO, this element rapidly decomposes and begins to smell.

MALE LOGIC

A man and his wife are in court getting a divorce. The problem is who should get custody of the child. The wife jumped up and said, " Your Honor, I brought a child into the world with pain and labor. She should be in my custody."

The Judge turns of the husband and says, "what do you have to say in your defense?"

The man sat for a while contemplating... slowly rose. "Your Honor, if I put a dollar in a vending machine and a Coke comes out... whose Coke is it... the machine's or mine?

LOVES

Loves to play. I love long walks in the woods, riding in your pickup truck, hunting, camping, and fishing trips, cozy winter nights lying by the fire. Candlelight dinners will leave me eating our of your hand. Rub me the right way and watch me respond. I'll be at the front door when you get home from work, wearing only what nature gave me. Kiss me and I'm yours.

Call xxx-xxxx and ask for "daisy". Over 150 me found themselves talking to the local Humane Society an 8 week old black Labrador retriever.

TAX TIME

The only thing the IRS has not yet taxed is the penis.
This is due to the fact that:
1. 40% of the time it is hanging around unemployed
2. 30% of the time it is hard up
3. 20% of the time it is pissed off
4. 10% or the time it's in the hole
5. It has 2 dependents but they're nuts
Effective January 1, 2011 penises will be taxed according
To size and the tax brackets are as follows:
10-12 inches Luxury Tax
8-10 inches Pole Tax
5-8 inches Privilege Tax
4-5 inches Nuisance Tax
Males exceeding 12 inches must file under Capitol Gains and anyone under 4 inches
Is eligible for a refund. The IRS asks that you please do not ask for an extension of any kind.
Please note:
Issues under considerations are as follows:
1. Are there penalties for early withdrawal?
2. Do multiple partners count as a corporation?
3. Are condoms deductible as work clothes?

DIFFERENCES

What is the difference between a girl friend and a wife?
45 pounds.

HOW TO SPEAK ABOUT WOMEN AND BE POLITICALLY CORRECT

1. She is not babe or a chick - She is a breasted American.
2. She is not a screamer or Moaner- She is vocally appreciative.
3. She is not easy- She is horizontally accessible.
4. She is not dumb-She is a detour off the information superhighway.
5. She has not been around- She is a previously enjoyed companion.
6. She is not an airhead- She is reality impaired.
7. She does not get drunk or tipsy- She gets chemically inconvenienced.
8. She is not horny- She is sexually focused.
9. she does not have breast implants- She is medically enhanced.
10. She does not nag you- She becomes verbally repetitive.
11. She is not a slut- She is sexually extroverted.
12. She does not have Major League Hooters- She is pectorally superior.
13. She is not a Two Bit Whore- She is a low cost provider.

HORMONE HOSTAGE

Every "Hormone Hostage" knows that there are days in the month when all a man has to do is oen his mouth and he takes his life in his hands. This is a handy guide that should be as common as a driver's license in the wallet of every husband, boyfriend or significant other.

Dangerous: What's for dinner?
Safer: Can I help you with dinner?
Safest: Where would you like to go for dinner?

Dangerous: Are you wearing THAT?
Safer: Gee, you look good in brown.
Safest: Wow! Look at you!

Dangerous: What are you so worked up about?
Safer: could we be overreacting?
Safest: Here's fifty dollars.

Dangerous: should you be eating that?
Safer: You know, there are a lot of apples left.
Safest: Can I get you a glass of wine with that?

Dangerous: what did you DO all day?
Safer: I hope you didn't overdo today.
Safest: I've always loved you in that robe.

DINNER WITH A FRIEND

A man was invited to a friend's home for dinner, where he noticed that his buddy preceded every request to his wife with endearing terms, calling her Honey, Darling, Sweetheart, Pumpkin, etc. He was impressed, since the couple had been married almost 70 years. While the wife was in the kitchen, he said, "I think it's wonderful that after all the years, you still call your wife those pet names." His buddy hung his head. "To tell you the truth, I forgot her name about 10 years ago.

THE PERFECT MAN

The perfect man is gentle
never cruel or mean.

He has a beautiful smile
and keeps his face so clean.
The perfect man likes children
And will raise them by your side.
He will be a good father
as well as a good husband to his bride.
The perfect man loves cooking
Cleaning and vacuuming too.
He'll do anything in his power
to convey his feelings of love on you.
The perfect man is sweet
writing poetry from your name.
He's a best friend to your mother
and kisses away your pain.
He never has made you cry
Or hurt you in any way.
Oh, ##%$ this stupid poem
The perfect man is gay

THE BITCHES

Three guys at a lady were sitting at the bar talking about their professions. The first guy says "I am Y.U.P.P.I.E., you know Young, Urban, Professional, Peaceful, Intelligent, Ecologist!"

The second guy says "I'm a D.I.N.K., you know ... Double Income , No , Kids."

The third guy says, "I'm a R.U.B., you know .. Rich, Urban, Biker."

They turned to the woman and asked her, "What are you?"

She replies: "I'm a WIFE, you know... Wash, Iron, F!@#, Etc." So, just exactly what is a
BITCH??????

CHAPTER 8 WOMEN AND MOTHER

THE SECRETS!

A Women's Five Essential Secrets to a Great Relationship:

1. It is important to find a man who works around the house, occasionally cooks and cleans, and who has a job.

2. It is important to find a man who makes you laugh.

3. It is important to find a man who's good in bed and who loves to have sex with you.

4. It is important to find a man who is dependable and doesn't lie.

5. It is important that you never let these four men meet each other.

MEN ARE LIKE.......

Men are like ... Laxatives ...They irritate the shit out of you. Men are like ... Bananas ... The older they get, the less firm they are. Men are like ... Vacations ... They never seem to be long enough. Men are like ... Weather ... Nothing can be done to change them. Men are like .... Blenders ... You need One, but you're not quite sure why. Men are like ... Chocolate Bars ... Sweet, smooth, & they usually head right for your hips. Men are like ... Coffee ... The best ones are rich, warm, & can keep you up all night long. Men are like ... Commercials ... You can't believe a word they say. Men are like ...Department Stores ... Their clothes are always 1/2 off. Men are like ....Government Bonds .... They take soooooooo long to mature. Men are like .... Mascara ... They usually run at the first sign of emotion. Men are like .... Popcorn ... They satisfy you, but, only for a little while. Men are like ...Snowstorms ... You never know when they're coming, how many inches you'll get or how long it will last. Men are like ... Lava Lamps ... Fun to look at, but not very bright. Men are like ... Parking Spots ... All the good ones are taken, the rest are handicapped

THE POLITICALLY CORRECT WAY...

She's not a chick or a babe -- she's a breasted American.

She's not half naked -- she's wardrobe impaired.

She's not conceited -- she's intimately aware of her best qualities.

She's not easy -- she's horizontally accessible.

She doesn't gain weight -- she's a metabolic underachiever.

She hasn't been around -- she's a previously enjoyed companion.

She doesn't flirt or tease -- she engages in artificial stimulation.

She doesn't turn you on -- she causes temporary blood displacement.

She doesn't wear to much perfume- she commits fragrance abuse.

She doesn't have a killer body - she's terminally attractive.

She's not kinky -- she's a non-inhibited sexual companion.

She doesn't get chubby or fat- she achieves maximum density.

She doesn't get tipsy or drunk -- she gets chemically inconvenienced.

She's not horny -- she's sexually focused.

She's not cold or frigid -- she's thermally inaccessible.

She doesn't wear to much makeup -- she reaches cosmetic saturation.

She doesn't have breast implants -- she's gravity resistant.

She doesn't nag you- She becomes verbally repetitive.

She's not a slut- she's sexually extroverted.
She's not loose -- she's morally impaired.
She does not have Major League Hooters -- she's pectorally superior.

MAKES SENSE

I never looked at it this way before:
MEN tal illness
MEN strual cramps
MEN tal breakdown
MEN opause
GUY necologist
HIS terectomy
Notice how all women's problems start with me

LADIES NIGHT CLUB

Last night, my friends and I went to a Ladies Night Club. One of the girls wanted to impress the rest of us, so she pulled out a $10 bill. When the male dancer came over to us, my friend licked the $10 bill and stuck it to his butt cheek! Not to be outdone, another friend pulls out a $20 bill. She called the guy back, licks the $20 bill, and sticks it to his other butt cheek. In another attempt to impress the rest of us, my third friend pulls out a $50 bill and calls the guy over, and licks the $50 bill. I'm worried about the way things are going, but fortunately, she just stuck it to one of his butt cheeks again. My relief was short-lived. Seeing the way things are going, the guy races over to me!!! Now everyone's attention is focused on me, and the guy is egging me on to try to top the $50. My brain was churning as I reached for my wallet...... What could I do?? The woman in me took over! I got out my ATM card, swiped it down the crack of his butt, grabbed the eighty bucks, and left.

CHICKEN SOUP

Martha Stewart's recipe for chicken casserole is quite efficient. First you boil the chicken in water. Then you dump the stock.

CHEMISTRY LESSON

Element Name: Womanium

Symbol: WO

Atomic Weight: Don't even go there

Physical Properties: Generally soft and round in form. Boils at nothing and may freeze any time. Melts when treated properly. Very bitter if not used well.

Chemical Properties: Very active. Highly unstable. Possesses strong affinity with gold, silver, platinum, and precious stones. Violent when left alone.

Able to absorb great amounts of exotic food. Turns slightly green when placed next to a better specimen.

Usage: Highly ornamental. An extremely good catalyst for dispersion of wealth.

Probably the most powerful income reducing agent known.

Caution : Highly explosive in inexperienced hands.

COMPUTER

A language instructor was explaining to her class that in French, nouns, like their English counterparts, are grammatically designated as masculine or feminine.

"House," in French is feminine- "la maison."

"Pencil," in French is masculine- "le crayon."

One puzzled student asked, "What gender is "computer"? The teacher did not know, and the word wasn't in her Fench dictionary. So for fun she split the class into two groups, appropriately enough, by gender and asked them to decide whether "computer' should be a masculine or feminine noun. Both groups were required to give four reasons for their Recommendation:

The men's group decided that computers should definitely be of the feminie gender

("la computer"), because:

1.No one but their creator understands their internal logic.

2. The native language they use to communicate with other computers is incomprehensible to everyone else.

3. Even the smallest mistakes are stored in long-term memory for possible later retrieval.

4. As soon as you make a commitment to one, you find yourself spending half your paycheck on accessories for it.

The women's group, however, concluded that computers should be masculine ("le computer"), because:

1. In order to get their attention, you have to turn them on.

2. They have a lot of data but they are still clueless.

3. They are supposed to help you solve problems, but half the time they are the problem.

4. As soon as you commit to one, you realize that if you'd waited a little longer, you could have gotten a better model.

The women won.

BIRTH CONTROL

What is the best form of birth control after 50?

Nudity.

DIFFERENCES MALE

What is the difference between a boyfriend and a husband?
45 minutes.

LIGHT BULB

How many women does it take to change a light bulb?
None, they just sit there and bitch.

MAN'S HEART

What is the fastest way to a man's heart?
Through his chest with a sharp knife.

FLOOR TILES

What do men and floor tiles got in common?
If you lay them properly the first time, you can walk all over them for life.

LOVES DIFFERENCES

What is the difference between a new husband and a new dog?
After a year, the dog is still excited to see you.

HOW TO SPEAK ABOUT MEN AND BE POLITICALLY CORRECT

1. He does not have a beer gut- He has developed a liquid grain storage facility.
2. He is not a bad dancer- He is overly Caucasian.
3. He does not get lost all the time- He investigates alternative destinations.
4. He is not balding- He is in follicle regression.

5. He is not a cradle robber- He prefers generationally differential relationships.

6. He does not get falling down drunk- He becomes accidentally horizontal.

7. he does not act like a total ass- He develops a case of rectal cranial inversion.

8. He is not a male chauvinist pig- He has swine empathy.

9. He is not afraid of commitment- He is monogamously challenged.

FIVE-STORY HOTEL

A group of girlfriends are on vacation when they see a five-story hotel with a sign that reads:

"For Women Only." Since they are without their boyfriends and husbands, they decide to go in.

The bouncer, a very attractive guy, explains to them how it works. "We have five floors. Go up floor by floor, and once you find what you are looking for, you can stay there. It's easy to decide since each floor has a sign telling you what's inside. So they start going up, and on the first floor the sign reads:"All the men on this floor are short and plain." The friends laugh, and without hesitation move onto the next floor. The sign on the second floor reads: "All the men here are short and handsome." Still, this isn't good enough, so the friends continue on up. They reach the third floor and the sign reads: "All the men here are tall and plain." They still want to do better, and so, knowing there are still two floors left, they kept going. On the fourth floor, the sign is perfect: "All the men here are tall and handsome." The women get excited and are about to go in when they realize that there is still one floor left. Wondering what they are missing, they head up to the fifth floor. There they find a sign that reads: "There are no men here. This floor was built only to prove that there is no way to please a woman."

TEN IS THE LIMIT

There were 11 people hanging on a single rope that suspended them from a helicopter trying to bring them to safety. Ten were men; one was a woman. They all decided that one person would have to let go because if they didn't, the rope would break and all them would die. No one could decide who is should be. Finally the woman gave a really touching speech, saying how she would give up her life to save the others, because women were used to giving things up for their husbands and children and giving in to men… All of the men started clapping.

LADIES ABOUT MEN

Don't imagine you can change a man – unless he's in diapers.

Go for younger men. You might as well- they never mature anyway.

Sadly, all men are created equal-they just have different faces so that you can tell them apart.

Best way to get a man to do something- suggest he's too old for it.

Love is blind, but marriage is a real eye-opener.

If you want a committed man, look in a mental hospital.

Remember a sense of humor does not mean you tell him jokes-it means you laugh at his.

The children of Israel wandered in the desert for 40 years-even in biblical times, men wouldn't ask for directions.

KUWAIT

A journalist had done a story on gender roles in Kuwait several years before Gulf War.

She noted then that women customarily walked about ten feet behind their husbands.

After the war, she returned to Kuwait and observed that now, the men were walking several yards behind their wives. She approached one of the women for an explanation.

"This is marvelous," said the journalist. "What enabled women here to achieve this reversal of roles?" replied the Kuwaiti woman, tersely: "Land mines."

WOMAN'S MEN ONE LINERS

What do you call a handcuffed man? Trustworthy

What does it mean when a man is in your bed gasping for breath and calling your name?

You didn't hold the pillow down long enough.

Why do only 10% of men make it to heaven? Because if they all went, it would be Hell.

Why do men like smart women? Opposites attract.

How do men exercise on the beach? By sucking in their stomachs every time they see a bikini.

How do you get a man to stop biting his nails? Make him wear shoes.

How does a man show he's planning for the future? He buys two cases of beer instead of one.

How many men does it take to screw in a light bulb? One.. he just holds it up and lets the world revolve around him.

What's the best way to force a man to do sit ups? Put the remote control between his toes.

ALL THE EQUIPMENT

A couple went on vacation to a fishing resort up North. The husband liked to fish at the crack of dawn; the wife preferred to read. One morning the husband returned after several hours of fishing and decided to take a short nap. The wife decided to take the boat out. She was not familiar with the lake so she rowed out, anchored the boat, and started reading her book. Along comes the sheriff in his boat, pulls up alongside and says, "Good morning, Ma'am. What are you doing?" "Reading my book," she replies as she thinks to herself, 'Is this guy blind or what?" "You're in a restricted area," he informs her. "But,

Officer, I'm not fishing. Can't you see that?" "But you have all this equipment, Ma'am. I'll have to take you in and write you up." "If you do that I will charge you with rape," snaps the irate woman. " I didn't even touch you," grouses the sheriff. "Yes, that's true.. but you have all the equipment…"

PUNCTUATION

An English professor wrote the words, "a woman without her man is nothing"

On the black board and directed the students to punctuate it correctly.

The men wrote: "A woman, without her man , is nothing."

The women wrote: "A woman: without her, man is nothing."

HOW TO IMPRESS A WOMAN/MAN

How To Impress A Woman:

Compliment her, respect her, honor her, cuddle her, kiss her, caress her, love her, stroke her, tease her, comfort her, protect her, hug her, hold her, spend money on her, wine and dine her, buy things for her, listened to her, care for her, stand by her, support her, hold her, go to the ends of the earth for her.

How to Impress A Man:

Show up naked. Bring food.

CHAPTER 9 CHILDREN

FIRST DAY OF SCHOOL IN 4TH GRADE

It was the first day of school and a new student named Martinez, the son of a Mexican restaurateur entered the fourth grade.

The teacher said, "Let's begin by reviewing some American history. Who said, "Give me liberty, or give me Death?"

She saw a sea of blank faces, except for Martinez, who had his hand up. "Patrick Henry, 1775."

"Very good! Who said "Government of the People, by the people, for the people, shall not perish from the earth"?

Again, no response except from Maritnez:

"Abraham Lincoln, 1863." said Martinez.

The teacher snapped at the class, "Class, you should be ashamed.

Martinez, who is new to our country, knows more about its history than you do."

She heard a loud whisper. "Screw the Mexicans."

"Who said that?" she demanded.

Martinex put his hand up "Jim Bowie, 1836."

At that point, a student in the back said, "I'm going to puke."

The teacher glares and asks "All right! Now. Who said that?"

Again, Martinez says, "George Bush to the Japanese Prime Minister, 1991."

Now furious, another student yells, "Oh yeah? Suck this!"

Martinez jumps out of his chair waving his hand and shouts to the teacher, "Bill Clinton, to Monica Lewinsky, 1997!"

Now with almost mob hysteria someone said, "You little shit. If you say anything else, I'll kill you."

Martinez frantically yells at the top of his voice, "Gary Condit to Chandra Levy 2001."

The teacher fainted. And as the class gathered around the teacher on the floor, someone said, "Oh shit, we're in BIG trouble!"

Martinez said, "Saddam Hussein 2003."

FIRST GRADE CLASS

A first grade teacher had twenty five students in her class. She presented each child

In her class the first half of a well known proverb and asked them to come up with the reminder of the proverb. These children are six year olds.

1. Don't change the horses….. until they stop running.
2. Strike while the ……..bug is close
3. It's always darkest before….Daylight Savings Time
4. Never underestimate the power of … termites.
5. You can lead a horse to water but.. how?
6. Don't bit the hand that… looks dirty.

First Grade Class continued:

7. No news is …. Impossible.
8. A miss is as good as a ………..Mr.
9. You can't teach an old dog new…. Math.
10. If you lie down with dogs, you'll …stink in the morning.
11. Love all, trust… me.
12. The pen is mightier than the …. Pigs.
13. An idle mind is … the best way to relax.
14. Where there's smoke there's …. Pollution.
15. Happy the bride who…. Gets all the presents.
16. A penny saved is … not much.
17. Two's company, three's…. the musketeers.
18. Don't put off till tomorrow what … you put on to go to bed.

19. Laugh and the whole world laughs with you , cry and .. you have to blow your nose.

20. there are non so blind as… Stevie Wonder.

21. Children should be seen and not… spanked or grounded.

22. If at first you don't succeed… get new batteries.

23. You get out of something only what you….see in the picture on the box.

24. When the blind lead the blind…. Get out of the way.

25. Better late than … pregnant.

BOX

VP Gore is out jogging one morning, notices a little boy on the corner with a box. Curious

He runs over to the child and says, "What's in the box kid?"

To which the little boy says, "Kittens, they're brand new kittens." Al gore laughs and says,

"What kind of kittens are they?" "Democrats," the child says. "Oh that's cute," Al says and he runs off.

A couple of days later Al is running with his buddy Bill Clinton and he spies the same boy with his box just ahead. Al says to Bill, "You got check this out" and they both jog over to the boy with the box. Al says, "Look in the box Bill, isn't that cute?" Look at those little kittens. Hey tell my friend Bill what kind of kittens they are."

The boy replies, "They're Republicans." "Whoa!" , Al says, "I came by here the other day and you said they were Democrats. What's up?" "Well," the kid says, "Their eyes are open now."

MEMORIAL DAY

Memorial Day weekend was coming up, and the nursery school teacher took the opportunity to tell her class about patriotism. "We live in a great country," she said. "One of the things we should be happy about is that, in this country, we are all free." One little boy came walking up to her from the back of the room. He stood with his hands on his hips and said, "I'm not free, I'm four.

GOOD EDUCATION

The young mother was very excited about studying philosophy; in fact, she was so enthusiastic about the life of the mind that she related everything to her studies. When she went to see the college's day care center with an eye to enrolling her toddler, she asked the woman in charge to outline its curriculum. "Well," responded the director with a twinkie, "today, for instance, we'll be studying the children's favorite philosopher: "Play-Doh."

CHAPTER 10 LAWYER

THE ISLAND

Two lawyers, Carl and Steve, decided to take their vacation together and went on a small, private plane to visit Paris for a time. There was a terrible storm, and the plane went down into the Atlantic ocean.

Fortunately, the two lawyers survived the crash, but had to swim to a nearby island that only had a few banana trees and and a few coconuts to live on. Each day, they would climb up the tallest tree to see if there was a ship out there to rescue them. One day, Carl called to Steve from from the tree, "I see a rubber raft!" And it's headed this way!" Steve called up, " Is there anyone in it?" "No.. Oh..wait! YES! It's a beautiful blonde women! And she's naked!" The rubber raft finally reached the tiny island, and the woman was alive, but unconscious. They pulled her up onto the beach, and Carl said, "It's been a real long time.. do you think we could you know..screw her?" Steve exclaimed,

"Out of what? That measly rubber raft?"

TEN TOP THINGS THAT SOUND DIRTY, BUT IN A LAW FIRM ARE NOT.

1. Have you looked through her briefs?
2. He is one hard judge.
3. Counselor, let's do it in chambers.
4. Her attorney withdrew at the last minute.
5. Is it a penal offence?
6. Better leave the handcuffs on.
7. For $200 an hour, she better be good.
8. Can you get him to drop his suit?
9. The judge gave her the stiffest one he could.
10. Think you can get me off?

YOUR HONOR

What do you throw a drowning lawyer? His partners.

What does a lawyer use for birth control? His personality.

What happens when you cross a pig with a lawyer? Nothing. There are some things a

pig won't do.

What is the difference between a lawyer and a vulture? The lawyer gets frequent flyer miles.

What's another difference between a lawyer and a vulture? Removable wingtips.

The post office just recalled their latest stamps. They had pictures of lawyers on them,

and people couldn't figure out which side to spit on.

How can a pregnant woman tell that she's carrying a future lawyer? She has

An uncontrollable craving for baloney.

How does a lawyer sleep? First he lies on one side, and then he lies on the other.

How many lawyers does it take to change a light bulb? How many can you afford?

How many lawyers does it take to screw in a light bulb? Three. One to climb the ladder, one to shake it, and one to sue the ladder company.

If a lawyer and an IRS agent were both drowning, and you could save only one of them, would you go to lunch or read the paper?

What did the lawyer name his daughter? Sue.

What do you call 25 skydiving lawyers? Skeet.
What do you call a lawyer gone bad? Senator.
What do you call a lawyer with an IQ of 50? Your Honor.
What do you get when you cross a bad politician with a crooked lawyer?
Chelsea Clinton.

ESTATE PLANNING

An elderly spinster called the lawyer's office and told the receptionist she wanted to see a lawyer about having a will prepared. The receptionist suggested they set up an appointment for a convenient time for the spinster to come into the office.

The woman replied, "You must understand, I've lived alone all my life, I rarely see anyone, and I don't like to go out. Would it be possible for the lawyer to come to my house?" The receptionist checked with the attorney who agreed and he went to the spinster's home for the meeting to discuss her estate and the will. The lawyer's first question was, "Would you please tell me what you have in assets and how you'd like them to be distributed under your will?" She replied, "Besides the furniture and accessories you see here, I have $40,000 in my savings account at the bank." "Tell me, " the lawyer asked, "how would you like the 40,000 to be distributed?" The spinster said, "Well, as I've told you, I've lived a reclusive life, people have hardly ever noticed me, so I'd like them to notice when I pass on. I'd like to provide $35,000 for my funeral." The lawyer remarked, "Well, for $35,000 you will be able to have a funeral that will certainly be noticed and will leave a lasting impression on anyone who may not have taken much note of you! But tell me," He continued, "What would you like to do with the remaining $5,000?" The spinster replied, "As you know, I've never married, I've lived alone almost my entire life, and in fact I've never slept with a man. Before I die, I'd like you to use the $5,000 to arrange for a man to sleep with me." "This is a very unusual request," the lawyer said, adding, "but I'll see what I can do to arrange it and get back to you." That evening, the lawyer was at home telling his wife about the eccentric spinster and her weird request. After thinking about how much she could do around the house with $5,000, and with a bit of coaxing, she got her husband to agree to provide the service himself. She said, "I'll drive you over tomorrow morning, and wait in the car until you're finished." The next morning, she drove him to the spinster's house and waited while he went into the house. She waited for over an hour, but her husband didn't come out. So she blew the car horn. Shortly, the upstairs bedroom window opened, the lawyer stuck his head out and yelled, "Pick me up tomorrow! She's going to let the County bury her!"

CYNICS DICTIONARY TERMS AND ONE LINER

Lawyer: A professional advocate hired to bend the law on behalf of a paying client; the reason considered the most suitable background for entry into politics.

CHAPTER 11 ONE LINER TYPES

SHORT ONE LINERS

If Barbie is so popular, why do you have to buy her friends?

Eagles may soar, but weasels don't get sucked into jet engines.

What happens if you get scared half to death twice?

My mechanic told me, "I couldn't repair your brakes, so I made your horn louder."

Why do psychics have to ask you for your name?

If at first you don't succeed, destroy all evidence that you tried.

A conclusion is the place where you got tired of thinking.

Experience is something you don't get until just after you need it.

The hardness of the butter is proportional to the softness of the bread.

To steal ideas from one person is plagiarism; to steal from many is research.

The problem with the gene pool is that there is no lifeguard.

The sooner you fall behind, the more time you'll have to catch up.

The colder the x-ray table, the more of your body is required to be on it.

Everyone has a photographic memory, some just don't have film.

SOMETHING TO PONDER IN ONE LINERS

Now that food has replaced sex in my life, I can't even get into my own pants.

Marriage changes passion. Suddenly you're in bed with a relative.

I saw a woman wearing a sweat shirt with "Guess" on it. So I said "Implants?" She hit me.

I don't do drugs. I get the same effect just standing up fast.

Sign in a Chinese Pet Store: "Buy one dog, get one flea..."

I live in my own little world. But it's OK. They know me here.

I got a sweater for Christmas. I really wanted a screamer or a moaner.

If flying is so safe, why do they call the airport the terminal?

I don't approve of political jokes. I've seen too many of them get elected.

There are two sides to every divorce: Yours and Shithead's.

I love being married. It's so great to find that one special person you want to annoy for the rest of your life.

I am a nobody, and nobody is perfect; therefore, I am perfect.

Every day I beat my own previous record for number of consecutive days I've stayed alive.

How come we choose from just two people to run for president and 50 for Miss America?

Isn't having a smoking section in a restaurant like having a peeing section in a swimming pool?

Why is it that most nudists are people you don't want to see naked?

Snowmen fall from Heaven unassembled.

Every time I walk into a singles bar I can hear Mom's wise words: "Don't pick that up, you don't know where it's been!"

A good friend will come and bail you out of jail...but, a true friend will be sitting next to you saying, "Damn...that was fun!"

He who laughs last, thinks slowest.

Everyone has a photographic memory. Some don't have film.

A day without sunshine I like, well night.

What does it mean when the flag at post office is flying at half mast? They're hiring.

NEWSPAPER HEADLINES 2035

Newspaper headlines in the year 2035Ozone created by electric cars now killing millions in the seventh largest country in the world, California. White minorities still trying to have English recognized as California's third language. Spotted Owl plague threatens northwestern United States crops & livestock. Baby conceived naturally.... Scientists stumped. Last remaining Fundamentalist Muslim dies in the American Territory of the Middle East (formerly known as Iran, Afghanistan, Syria, and Lebanon).North Korea still closed off; physicists estimate it will take at least ten more years before radioactivity decreases to safe levels. Castro finally dies at age 112; Cuban cigars can now be imported legally, but President Chelsea Clinton has banned all smoking. George Z. Bush says he will run for President in 2036. Postal Service raises price of first class stamp to $17.89 and reduces mail delivery to Wednesday only. 35 year study: Diet and Exercise is the key to weight loss. Massachusetts executes last remaining conservative. Supreme Court rules punishment of criminals violates their civil rights. Average height of NBA players now nine feet, seven inches. New federal law requires that all nail clippers, screwdrivers, fly swatters, and rolled up newspapers must be registered by January 2036. Congress authorizes direct deposit of illegal political contributions to campaign account . Capitol Hill intern indicted for refusing to have sex with congressman. IRS sets lowest tax rate at 75%. Florida Democrats still don't know how to use a voting machine.

KIND A DIFFERENT

My husband and I divorced over religious differences. He thought he was God and I didn't. I don't suffer from insanity; I enjoy every minute of it. I work hard because millions on welfare depend on me. Some people are alive only because it's illegal to kill them. I used to have a handle on life, but it broke. Don't take life too seriously -- no one gets out alive. You're just jealous because the voices only talk to me.

Beauty is in the eye of the beer holder. Earth is the insane asylum for the universe. Quoting one is plagiarism; quoting many is research. I'm not a complete idiot -- some parts are missing.Out of my mind. Back in five minutes. Nyquil, the stuffy, sneezy, why-the-heck-is-the-room-spinning medicine. God must love stupid people, He made so many. The gene pool could use a little chlorine. It IS as BAD as you think and they ARE out to get you. Consciousness: that annoying time between naps. Ever stop to think and forget to start again? MOP AND GLOW - Floor wax used by Three Mile Island cleanup crew. Being "over the hill" is much better than being under it.

Wrinkled was not one of the things I wanted to be when I grew up.

Procrastinate Now!

My dog can lick anyone! I have a degree in liberal arts; do you want fries with that? FAILURE IS NOT AN OPTION. It comes bundled with the software. A hangover is the wrath of grapes. A journey of a thousand miles begins with a cash advance. STUPIDITY IS NOT A HANDICAP. Park elsewhere! They call it PMS because Mad Cow Disease was already taken.

He who dies with the most toys is nonetheless dead. A PICTURE IS WORTH A THOUSAND WORDS, but it uses up three thousand times the memory on your computer.HAM AND EGGS -- A day's work for a chicken, a lifetime commitment for a pig. The trouble with life is there's no background music.

TEN TOP THINGS ABOUT GOLF THAT SOUND DIRTY BUT AREN'T

1. Damn my shaft is bent.
2. After 18 holes, I can barely walk.
3. You really whacked the hell out of that sucker.
4. Look at the size of his putter.
5. Keep your head down and spread your legs a bit more.
6. Mind if I join your threesome?
7. Stand with your back turned and drop it.
8. My hands are so sweaty I can't get a good grip.
9. Nice stroke, but your follow-through leaves a lot to be desired.
10. Hold up! I need to wash my balls first.

TEN TOP THINGS THAT SOUND DIRTY IN THE OFFICE BUT AREN'T

1. I need to whip it out by 5.
2. Mind if I use your laptop?
3. Just stick it in my box.
4. If I have to lick one more, I'll gag.
5. I want it on my desk, NOW!
6. HMMM, I think it's out of fluid.
7. My equipment is so old, it takes forever to finish.
8. It's an entry level position.
9. When do you think you'll be getting off today?
10. It's not fair. I do all the work while he just sits there!

PUNS INTENDED

What do you call a boomerang that doesn't work? A Stick.
What do you call cheese that isn't yours? Nacho Cheese.
What do you call Santa's helpers? Subordinate Clauses.

What do you get when you cross a snowman with a vampire? Frostbite.

What lies at the bottom of the ocean and twitches? A nervous wreck.

What is the difference between roast beef and pea soup? Anyone can roast beef.

What kind of coffee was served on the Titanic? Sanka.

What is the difference between a Harley and a Hoover? The location of the dirt bag.

PICKUPS LINERS AND RESPONSES

Man: "Haven't we met before?"
Woman: "Yes, I'm the receptionist at the V.D. clinic."

Man: "Haven't I seen you somewhere before?"
Woman: "Yeah, that's why I don't go there anymore."

Man: "Is this seat empty?"
Woman: "Yes, and this one will be too if you sit down."

Man: "So, wanna go back to my place?"
Woman: "Well, I don't know. Will tow people fit under a rock?"

Man: "Your place or mine?"
Woman: "Both. You go to yours and I'll go to mine."

Man: "I'd really like to get into your pants."
Woman: "No thanks. There's already one asshole in there."

Man: "I'd like to call you. What's your number?"
Woman: "It's in the phone book."

Man : "But I don't know your name."
Woman: 'That's in the phone book too."

Man: "So what do you do for a living?"
Woman: " I'm a female impersonator."

Man: "Voulez-vous coucher avec mo ice soir?"
(Would you like to go to bed with me tonight?)
Woman: "Je voudrais bien, mais je n'ai rien a porter."
(I would love to , but I have nothing to wear.)

Man: "What sign were you born under?"
Woman: "No parking."

Man: "Hey, baby, what's your sign?"
Woman: "Do not enter" (or) "Stop."

Man: "How do you like your eggs in the morning?"
Woman: "Unfertilized!"

Man: "Hey, come on, we're both here at this bar for the same reason."
Woman: "Yeah! Let's pick up some chicks!"

Man: "I'm here to fulfill your every sexual fantasy."
Woman: "You mean you've got both a donkey and a Great Dane?"

Man: "I know how to please a woman."
Woman: "then please leave me alone."

Man: "I want to give myself to you."
Woman: "Sorry, I don't accept cheap gifts."

Man: "I can tell that you want me."
Woman: "Ohhh. You're so right I want you to leave."

Man: " If I could see you naked, I'd die happy."
Woman: "Yeah, but if I saw you naked, I'd probably die laughing."

Man: "Hey cutie, how 'bout you and I hitting the hot spots?"
Woman: "Sorry, I don't date outside my species."

Man: "May I see you pretty soon?"
Woman: "Why? Don't you think I'm pretty now?"

Man: "Your body is like a temple."
Woman: "Sorry, there are no services today."

Man: "I'd go through anything for you."
Woman: "Good! Let's start with your bank account."

Man: "I would go to the end of the world for you."
Woman: "Yes, but would you stay there."

STOCK MARKET TERMINOLOGY DICTIONARY OF THE PAST

Momentum Investing-The fine art of buying high and selling low.

Value Investing- The art of buying low and selling lower.

Broker- Poorer than you were in 1999.

P/E ratio- The percentage of investors wetting their pants as this market keeps crashing.

Standard & Poor- Your life in a nut shell.

Stock Analyst- Idiot who just downgraded your stock.

Bull Market- a random market movement causing an investor to mistake himself for a financial genius.

Bear Market- a 6 to 18 month period when the kids get no allowance, the wife gets no jewelry and the husband gets no sex.

Stock Split- when your ex-wife and her lawyer split all your assets equally between themselves.

Financial Planner- A guy who actually remembers his wallet when he runs to the 7-11 for toilet paper and cigarettes.

Market correction- The day after you buy stocks.

Cash Flow- The movement your money makes as it disappears down the toilet.

Call Option- Something people used to do with a telephone in ancient times before e-mail.

Cisco- Side kick of Poncho.

Yahoo- What you yell after selling it to some poor sucker for $540 per stake.

Window 2000- What you jump out of when you're the sucker that bought Yahoo at $540 per share.

Institutional Investor- Past year investor who's now locked up in a nut house.

Profit- Religious guy who talks to G-d.

Bill Gates- Where G-d goes for a loan

Alan Green span- G-d for awhile.

REGULAR ONE LINERS

Change is inevitable, except from a vending machine.

I just got lost in thought, in other words I was in unfamiliar territory.

When the chips are down, the buffalo is empty.

Seen it all, done it all, can't remember most of it.

Those who live by the sword get shot by those who don't.

I feel like I'm diagonally parked in a parallel universe.

You have the right to remain silent, in other words, anything you say will be misquoted and then used against you.

I wonder how much deeper the ocean would be without sponges.

Two cannibals are eating a clown. One says to the other, "Does this taste funny to you?"

I went to buy some camouflage trousers the other day but couldn't find any.

Honk if you love peace and quiet.

Nothing is foolproof to a sufficiently talented fool.

It is hard to understand how a cemetery raised its burial cost and blamed it on the cost of living.

You have the right to remain silent. Anything you way willb e misquoted, then used against you.

I wonder how deep the ocean would be without sponges.

The 50-50-90 rule; Anytime you have a 50-50 chance of getting something right, there's a 90% probability you'll get it wrong.

Everybody lies, but it doesn't matter if nobody listens.

I wish the buck stopped here, I could have a few.

I started out with nothing, and I still have most of it.

Light travels faster than sound. This is why some people appear brighter until yo hear them speak.

A fine is a tax for doing wrong. A tax is a fine for doing well.

NOW THAT I'M OLDER I HAVE DISCOVERED

I started out with nothing, and I still have most of it.

My wild oats have turned into prunes and All Bran.

I finally got my head together, now my body is falling apart.

Funny, I don't remember being absent minded.

All reports are in, life is now officially unfair.

If all is not lost, where is it?

It is easier to get older than it is to get wiser.

Some days you're the dog, some days you're the hydrant.

I wish the buck stopped here, I sure could use a few.

Kids in the back seat cause accidents.

Accidents in the back seat cause kids.

It's hard to make a comeback when you haven't been anywhere.

Only time the world beats a path to your door is when you're in the bathroom.

If god wanted me to touch my toes, he would have put them on my knees.

When I'm finally holding all the cards, why does everyone decide to play chess?

It's not hard to meet expenses, they're everywhere.

The only difference between a rut and a grave is the depth.

These days, I spend a lot of time thinking about the hereafter… I go somewhere to get

Something and then wonder what I'm here after.

RIDDLE

What color is rain?

Watercolor of course.

PREREQUISITES OF A GOOD DEMOCRAT

You have to believe the AIDS virus is spread by a lack of federal funding.

You have to believe that the same teacher who can't teach 4th graders how to read is somehow qualified to teach the same kids about sex.

You have to believe that guns, in the hands of law-abiding Americans , are more of a threat than U.S. nuclear weapons technology in the hands of Chinese communists.

You have to believe that global temperatures are less affected by cyclical, documented changes in the earth's climate, and more affected by yuppies driving SUV's.

You have to believe that gender roles are artificial but being homosexual is natural.

You have to be against capital punishment but support abortion on demand.

You have to believe that businesses create oppression and governments create prosperity.

You have to believe that hunters don't care about nature, but loony activists who have never been out Seattle do.

You have to believe that self-esteem is more important than actually doing something to earn it.

You have to believe the military, not corrupt politicians, start wars.

You have to believe that NRA is bad, because it supports certain parts of the Constitution, while the ACLU is good, because it supports certain parts of the Constitution.

You have to believe that taxes are too low, but ATM fees are too high.

You have to believe that self-esteem is more important than actually doing something to earn it.

CHAPTER 12 FATHER

DADDY'S DATING RULES

Rule One:

If you pull into my driveway and honk you'd better be delivering a package, because you're sure not picking anything up.

Rule Two:

You do not touch my daughter in front of me. You may glance at her, so long as you do not peer at anything below her neck. If you cannot keep your eyes or hands off of my daughter's body, I will remove them.

Rule Three:

I am aware that it is considered fashionable for boys of your age to wear their trousers so loosely that they appear to be falling off their hips. Please don't take this as an insult, but you and all Of your friends are complete idiots. Still, I want to be fair and open minded bout this issue, so I propose this compromise: You may come to the door with your underwear showing and your pants ten sizes too big, and I will not object. However, in order to ensure that your clothes do not, in fact come off during the course of your date with my daughter, I will take my electric nail gun and fasten your trousers securely in place to your waist.

Rule Four:

I'm sure you've been told that in today's world, sex without utilizing a "Barrier Method" of some kind can kill you. Let me elaborate: when it comes to sex, I am the barrier, and I will kill you.

Rule Five:
It is usually understood that in order for us to get to know each other, we should talk about sports, politics, and other issues of the day. Please do not do this. The only information I require from you is an indication of when you expect to have my daughter safely back at my house, and the only word I need from you on this subject is : "early."

Rule Six:
I have no doubt you are a popular fellow, with many opportunities to date other girls. This is fine with me as long as it is okay with my daughter. Otherwise, once you have gone out with my little girl, you will continue to date no one but her until she is finished with you. If you make her
cry, I will make you cry.

Rule Seven:
As you stand in my front hallway, waiting for my daughter to appear, and more than an hour goes by, do not sigh and fidget. If you want to be on time for the movie, you should not be dating.
My daughter is putting on her makeup, a process that can take longer than painting the Golden Gate Bridge. Instead of just standing there, why don't you do something useful, like changing the oil in my car?

Rule Eight:
The following places are not appropriate for a date with my daughter. Places where there are beds, sofas, or anything softer than a wooden stool. Places where there is darkness. Places where there is dancing holding hands, or happiness. Places where the ambient temperature is warm enough to induce my daughter to wear shorts, tank tops, midriff T-shirts, or anything other than

Overalls, a sweater, and a goose down parka- zipped up to her throat. Movies with a strong romantic or sexual theme are to be avoided; movies which features chain saws are okay. Hockey games are okay. Old folks homes are better.

Rule Nine:
Do not lie to me. I may appear to be a potbellied, balding, middle-aged, dimwitted has-been. But on issues relating to my daughter, I am the all-knowing, merciless god of your universe. If I ask you where you are going and with whom, you have one chance to tell me the truth, the whole truth and nothing but the truth. I have a shotgun, a shovel , and five acres behind the house. Do not trifle with me.

Rule Ten:
Be afraid, be very afraid. It takes very little for me to mistake the sound of our car in the driveway for a chopper coming in over a rice paddy near Hanoi. When my Agent Orange starts Acting up, the voices in my head frequently tell me to clean the guns as I wait for you to bring my daughter home. As soon as you pull into the driveway, you should exit the car with both hands in plain sight. Speak the perimeter password, announce in a clear voice that you have brought my daughter home safely and early, then return to your car- there is no need for you to come inside. The camouflaged face at the window is mine.

THE LETTERS
Dear Dad,
$chool i$ really great. I am making lot$ of friend$ and $tudying very hard.

With all my $tuff, I $imply can't think of anything I need, $o if you would like, you can jus$t $end me a card, a$ I would love to hear from you.

Love,

Your $on

The Reply:

Dear Son,

I kNOw that astronomy, economics, and oceanography are eNOugh to keep even and hoNOr

Student busy. Do NOt forget that the pursuit of kNOwledge is a NOble task, and you can never study eNOugh.

Love ,

Dad

CHAP 13 CALIFORNIA AND OTHER STATES

MINNESOTA

You know you are a true Minnesotan when: Your idea of a traffic jam is ten cars waiting to pass a tractor on the highway."Vacation" means going up north past Brainerd for the weekend. You measure distance in hours. You know several people who have hit deer more than once. You often switch from "heat" to "A/C" in the same day and back again. Your whole family wears Viking purple to church on Sunday. You can drive 65 mph through 2 feet of snow during a raging blizzard, without flinching. You see people wearing hunting clothes at social events. You install security lights on your house and garage and leave both unlocked. You think of the major food groups as beer, fish, and venison. You carry jumper cables in your car and your girlfriend knows how to use them. There are 7 empty cars running in the parking lot at Mill's Fleet Farm at any given time. You design your kid's Halloween costume to fit over a snowsuit. Driving is better in the winter because the potholes are filled with snow. You refer to the Vikings as "we."You know all 4 seasons: almost winter, winter, still winter and road construction. You can identify a southern or eastern accent. You have no problem pronouncing Wayzata. You consider Minneapolis exotic. You don't have a coughing fit from one sip of Pig's Eye Pilsner. Your idea of creative landscaping is a statue of a deer next to your blue spruce. You were unaware that there is a legal drinking age. Down South to you means Iowa. A brat is something you eat. Your neighbor throws a party to celebrate his new machine shed. You go out to fish fry every Friday.

You know how to polka. Your 4th of July picnic was moved indoors due to frost. You have more miles on your snow blower than your car. You find 0 degrees "a little chilly."You actually understand these jokes, and you forward them to all your Minnesota friends.

YOU KNOW YOU'RE FROM CALIFORNIA IF :

1. Your co-worker has 8 body piercings and none are visible. 2. You make over $300,000 and still can't afford a house. 3. You take a bus and are shocked at two people carrying on a conversation in English. 4. Your child's 3rd-grade teacher has purple hair, a nose ring, and is named Breeze. 5. You can't remember . . . is pot illegal? 6. You've been to a baby shower that has two mothers and a sperm donor. 7. You have a very strong opinion about where your coffee beans are grown, and you can taste the difference between Sumatran and Ethiopian. 9. You can't remember . . . is pot illegal? 10. A really great parking space can totally move you to tears.11. A low speed police pursuit will interrupt ANY TV broadcast. 12. Gas costs $1.00 per gallon more than anywhere else in the U.S. 13. Which proposition is it this year? 14. Unlike back home, the guy at 8:30 am at Starbucks' wearing the baseball cap and sunglasses who looks like George Clooney really IS George Clooney. 15. Your car insurance costs as much as your house payment. 16. Your hairdresser is straight, your plumber is gay, the woman who delivers your mail is into S & M. 17. Your Mary Kay rep is a guy in drag.18. It's barely sprinkling rain and there's a report on every news station: "STORM WATCH". 19. You pass an elementary school playground and the children are all busy with their cells or pagers. 20. It's barely sprinkling rain outside, so you leave for work an hour early to avoid all the weather-related accidents . . .21. Both you AND your dog have therapists . . . and lastly, 22. The Terminator is your governor.

GEOGRAPHY LESSON:

YOU LIVE IN ARIZONA WHEN...

1. You are willing to park 3 blocks away because you found shade.

2. You can open and drive your car without touching the car door or the steering wheel.

3. You've experienced condensation on your butt from the hot water in the toilet bowl.

4. You would give anything to be able to splash cold water on your face.

5. You can attend any function wearing shorts and a tank top.

6. "Dress Code" is meaningless at high schools and universities. Picture lingerie ads.

7. You can drive for 4 hours in one direction and never leave town.

8. You have over 100 recipes for Mexican food.

9. The 4 seasons are: tolerable, hot, really hot, and ARE YOU KIDDING ME??!!

10. You know that "dry heat" is comparable to what hits you in the face when you open your oven door.

YOU LIVE IN CALIFORNIA WHEN...

1. You make over $250,000 and you still can't afford to buy a house.

2 The high school quarterback calls a time-out to answer his cell phone.

3. The fastest part of your commute is going down your driveway.

4. You know how to eat an artichoke.

5. You drive your rented Mercedes to your neighborhood block party.

6. When someone asks you how far something is, you tell them how long it will take to get there rather than how many miles away it is.

YOU LIVE IN NEW YORK CITY WHEN...

1. You say "the city" and expect everyone to know you mean Manhattan.

2. You have never been to the Statue of Liberty or the Empire State Building.

3. You can get into a four-hour argument about how to get from Columbus Circle to Battery Park, but can't find Wisconsin on a map.

4. You think Central Park is "nature,"

5. You believe that being able to swear at people in their own language makes you multi-lingual.

6. You've worn out a car horn.

7. You think eye contact is an act of aggression.

YOU LIVE IN MAINE WHEN...

1. You only have four spices: salt, pepper, ketchup, and Tabasco.

2. Halloween costumes fit over parkas.

3. You have more than one recipe for moose.

4. Sexy lingerie is anything flannel with less than eight buttons.

5. The four seasons are: winter, still winter, almost winter, and construction.

YOU LIVE IN THE DEEP SOUTH WHEN...

1. You can rent a movie and buy bait in the same store.

2."ya'll" is singular and "all ya'll" is plural.

3. After five years you still hear, "You ain't from 'round here, are Ya?"

4. "He needed killin' " is a valid defense.

5. Everyone has 2 first names: Billy Bob, Jimmy Bob, Mary Sue, Betty Jean, Mary Beth, Bobbie Sue, Billie Joe, etc.

YOU LIVE IN COLORADO WHEN...

1. You carry your $3,000 mountain bike atop your $500 car.

2... You tell your husband to pick up Granola on his way home and he stops at the day care center.

3. A pass does not involve a football or dating.

4. The top of your head is bald, but you still have a pony tail.

YOU LIVE IN THE MIDWEST WHEN...

1. You've never met any celebrities, but the mayor knows your name.

2. Your idea of a traffic jam is ten cars waiting to pass a tractor.

3. You have had to switch from "heat" to "A/C" on the same day.

4. You end sentences with a preposition: "Where's my coat at?"

5. When asked how your trip was to any exotic place, you say, "It was different!"

YOU LIVE IN FLORIDA WHEN....

1. You eat dinner at 3:15 in the afternoon.

2. All purchases include a coupon of some kind -- even houses and cars.

3. Everyone can recommend an excellent dermatologist.
4. Road construction never ends anywhere in the state.
5. Cars in front of you are often driven by headless people.

CALIFORNIA STARS ON MUSIC

Steven Spielberg was discussing his new project. It's a drama about
famous composers, starring top stars. Sylvester Stallone, Steven Segal,
Bruce Willis and Arnold Schwarzenegger were all present. Spielberg was prepared
to allow them to select whatever composers they would portray, as long
as they were very famous. "Well," started Stallone, "I've always admired Mozart. I would love
to play him." "Chopin has always been my favorite, and my image would improve if people saw
me playing the piano," said Willis. "I've always been partial to Strauss and
his waltzes," said Segal. Spielberg was very pleased with these choices. "Sounds
splendid." Then, looking at Schwarzenegger, he asked, "Who do you want to
be, Arnold?" So Arnold said, "I'll be Bach."

GREATER LOS ANGELES AREA DRIVERS LICENSE APPLICATION

This is a new exam. Since driving conditions and culture are unique in Los Angeles, you may not have realized that the California Department of Motor Vehicles has now issued a special application and driver's test solely for the Los Angeles Metropolitan area.

Name:_____ Stage name:_____
Agent:_____ Attorney:_____
Therapist name:_____
Sex:__male___female__formerly   male____formerly
female_____ both___
*If female, indicate breast implant size:_____
Will the size of your implants hinder your ability to safely operate a motor vehicle
In any way? Yes__ No__
Please list brand name of cell phone:_____
*If   you   don't   own   a   cell   phone   please
explain:_____
Please check hair color:
Females:[ ]Blonde [ ] Platinum Blonde
Teenagers:[ ]Red [ ]Orange [ ] Green [ ] Purple [ ] Blue [ ]
Skinhead [ ].
Please check activities you perform while driving: (Check all that apply)
[ ] Eating
[ ] Drinking Starbucks Coffee
[ ] Applying make-up
[ ] Shaving (male or female)
[ ] Talking on the phone
[ ] Texting
[ ] Dragon point and speak
[ ] Slapping kids in the back seat
[ ] Applying cellulite treatment to thighs
[ ] Tanning
[X] Snorting cocaine (already checked for your convenience)
[ ] watching TV
[ ] Reading Variety
[ ] Surfing the net via laptop
[ ] discharging firearms/Reloading

Please indicate how many times:
a) you expect to shoot at other drivers___
b) how many times you expect to be shot at while driving__
If you are the victim of a carjacking, you should immediately:
a) call the police to report the crime
b) Call Channel 9 News to report the crime, then watch your car on the news in a
     high-speed chase
c) Call your attorney and discuss lawsuit against cellular phone company
d) Call your therapist
In the event of an earthquake, you should:
a) Stop your car
b) keep driving and hope for the best
c) immediately use your cell phone to call all loved ones.
d) pull out your video camera and obtain footage for Channel 9
In the instance of rain you should:
a) never drive over 5MPH
b) drive twice as fast as usual.
c) you're not sure what "rain" is.
Please indicate number of therapy sessions per week:
Are you presently taking any of the following medications?
a)Prozac
b)Zovirax
c)Lithium
d)Zanax
e)Valium
f)Zoloft
g) All of the above
h)None of the above
*If none, please explain:_____.
Length of daily commute:

a)Less than 1 hour
b) 1 hour
c) 2 hours
d) 3 hours
e)4hours
*If less than 1 hour, please explain:_____.
When Stopped by police, you should?
a)pull over and have your driver's license and insurance form ready.
b)have your video camera ready and provoke them to attack, thus ensure yourself of a hefty lawsuit.
When turning, you should always signal your intentions by:
a)using your directional signals.
b)what is a "directional signal"?
Which part of your car will wear out most often?
a)the wiper blades
b)the belts
c)horn
The "bright" setting on your headlights is for:
a)dark, poorly lit roads
b)flashing to get the car ahead to move out of the way
c)revenge!
Your rear view mirror is for :
a)watching for approaching cars
b)watching for approaching police cars
c)checking your hair

RULES FOR CALIFORNIA DRIVERS

1. Turn signals will give away your next move. A real California driver never uses them.

2. Under no circumstances should you leave a safe distance between you and the car in

Front of you, If you do the space will be filled by somebody else who will flip you Off.

3. Crossing two or more lanes in a single lane change is considered going with the flow.

4. The faster you drive through a red light, the smaller the chance you have of getting hit.

5. Never, ever come to a complete stop at a stop sign. No one expects it and it will inevitably result in you being rear-ended. If you want your insurance company to pay

For a new rear bumper, come to a complete stop at all stop signs.

6. A right lane construction closure is just a game to see how many people can cut in line by passing you on the right as you sit in the left lane waiting for the same jerks to squeeze their way back in before hitting the orange and white barricades.

7. Braking is to be done as hard and late as possible to ensure that your ABS kicks in, giving a nice, relaxing foot massage as the brake pedal pulsates. For those of you

Without ABS, it's a chance to stretch your legs.

8. Never pass on the left when you can pass on the right. It's a good way to scare people entering the highway.

9. Speed limits are arbitrary figures, given only as suggestions and are apparently not enforceable in the California during rush hour.

10. Just because you're in the left lane and have no room to speed up, or move over doesn't mean that a California driver flashing his high beams behind you doesn't think he can go faster in your spot.

11. Please remember that there is no such thing as a shortcut during rush-hour traffic in California.

12. Always slow down and rubberneck when you see an accident or even someone changing a tire.

13. Learn to swerve abruptly. California is the home of high-speed slalom driving thanks to the Caltrans, which put potholes in key locations to test drivers' reflexes and keep them on their toes.

14. It is traditional in California to honk your horn at cars that don't move the instant the light changes.

15. Never take a green light at face value. Always look right and left before proceeding.

16. Remember that the goal of every California driver is to get there first, by whatever means necessary.

17. Real California female drivers can put on pantyhose and apply eye makeup at seventy-five miles per hour or in bumper-to-bumper traffic.

18. Real California male drivers can remove their girlfriend's panties and bra at Seventy-five miles per hour or in bumper-to-bumper traffic.

19. In California, flipping someone the bird is considered a California salute. This gesture should always be returned.

20. Never pay attention to a "Yield" sign. It is the responsibility of those who are already in the lane to watch for you and anticipate you gunning into traffic.

21. If you are a recent immigrant to the United States, you are allowed to drive where ever and however you please. We're just so damn happy to have you here, we'll be willing to stay out of your way!

SUMMER IN PALM SPRINGS CALIFORNIA

We know summer has arrived in Palm Springs, California when:

The best parking place is determined by shade instead of distance.

How water comes out of both taps.

You can make instant sun tea.

You learn that a seat belt makes a pretty dam good branding iron.

The temperature drops below 95 and you feel a bit chilly.

You discover it takes only 2 fingers to drive your car.

You discover you can get sunburn through your car windows.

You need a potholder to open your car door.

Your biggest bicycle wreck fear is: What if I get knocked out and end up lying on the

pavement to cook to death.

You recognize asphalt in its liquid state.

The birds are using potholders to pull worms out of the ground.

The potatoes cook underground and all you have to do is pull them out and add butter.

Farmers are putting crushed ice in their chicken's nests to keep them from laying hard boiled eggs.

The cows are giving evaporated milk.

The trees are whistling for dogs.

STATE SLOGANS

Alabama: Yes, we have electricity

Alaska: 11,623 Eskimos can't be wrong!

Arizona: But it's a dry heat

Arkansas: Literacy ain't everything

California: By 30, our women have more plastic than your Honda

Colorado: If you don't ski, don't bother

Connecticut: Like Massachusetts, only the Kennedy's don't own it.

Delaware: We Really do like the chemicals in our water

Florida: Ask us about our grandkids

Georgia: We put the "Fun" in fundamentalist extremism

Hawaii: Haka Tiki Mou Sha'ami Leeki Toru (Death to mainland scrum, but leave your money)

Idaho: More than just potatoes.. well okay, we're not, but the potatoes sure are real good

Illinois: Please don't pronounce the "S"

Indiana: 2 billion years tidal wave free

Iowa: We do amazing things with corn

Kansas: first of the Rectangle states

Kentucky: five million people, fifteen last names

Louisiana: we're not all drunk Cajun wackos, but that's our tourism campaign

Maine: We're really cold, but we have cheap lobster

Maryland: If you can dream it, we can tax it

Massachusetts: Our taxes are lower than Sweden't (for most tax brackets)

Michigan: first Line of defense from the Canadians

Minnesota: 10,000 lakes… and 10,000,000,000,000 mosquitoes

Mississippi: come and feel better about your own state

Missouri: Your federal flood relief tax dollars at work

Montana: Land of the big sky, the Unabomber, right-wing crazies, and very little else

Nebraska: Ask about our state motto contest

Nevada: Whores and poker!

New Hampshire: go away and leave us alone

New Jersey: You want a ##$%## motto? I got yer ##$%##! Motto right here

New Mexico: lizards make excellent pets

New York: You have the right to remain silent, you have the right to an attorney

North Carolina: Tobacco is a vegetable

North Dakota: We really are one of the 50 states

Ohio: At least we're not Michigan
Oklahoma: Like the play, only no singing
Oregon: Spotted Owl .. it's what's for dinner
Pennsylvania: Cook with coal
Rhode Island: We're not really an island
South Carolina: Remember the Civil War! We didn't really surrender
South Dakota: Closer than North Dakota
Tennessee: The Education state
Texas: Si hablo Ing'les (Yes, I speak English)
Utah: Our Jesus Is better that your Jesus
Vermont : Yep
Virginia: Who says government stiffs and slackjaw yokels don't mix.
Washington, D.C.: Wanna be Mayor?
West Virginia: One big happy family.. really
Wisconsin: Come cut the cheese
Wyoming: Where men are men and sheep are scared

COLORADO STATE FISH AND WILDLIFE

The Colorado State Department of Fish and Wildlife is advising hikers, hunter, fishers, and golfers to take extra precautions and keep alert for bears while in the Dillon,

Breckenridge, and Keystone area. They advise people to wear noise-producing devices such as little bells on their clothing to alert, but not startle the bears unexpectedly.

They also advise the carrying of pepper spray in case of an encounter with a bear. It is also a good idea to watch for fresh signs of bear activity. People should recognize the difference between black bear and grizzly bear droppings. Black bear droppings are smaller and contain berries and possibly squirrel fur. Grizzly bear droppings have little bells in them and smell like pepper spray.

QUICK AND EASY WAYS TO IDENTIFY DRIVERS' HOME TOWN

One hand on the wheel, one hand on horn: Chicago.

One hand on wheel, one finger out window: New York.

One hand on wheel, one hand on newspaper, foot solidly on Accelerator: Boston.

One hand on wheel, cradling cell phone, brick on accelerator: California.

With gun in lap: Los Angeles, California.

Both hands on wheel, eyes shut, both feet on break, quivering in terror: Ohio; but driving in California.

Both hands in air, gesturing, both feet on accelerator, head turned to talk to someone in back seat: Italy.

CHAPTER 14 ARTIST

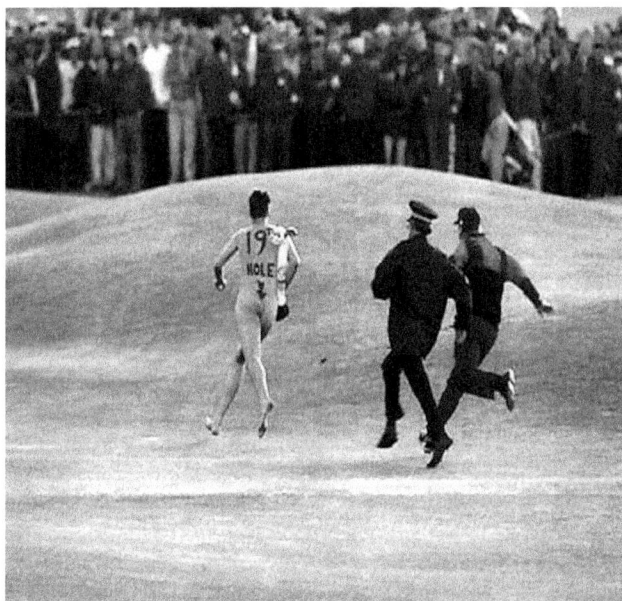

Aftican Taxi

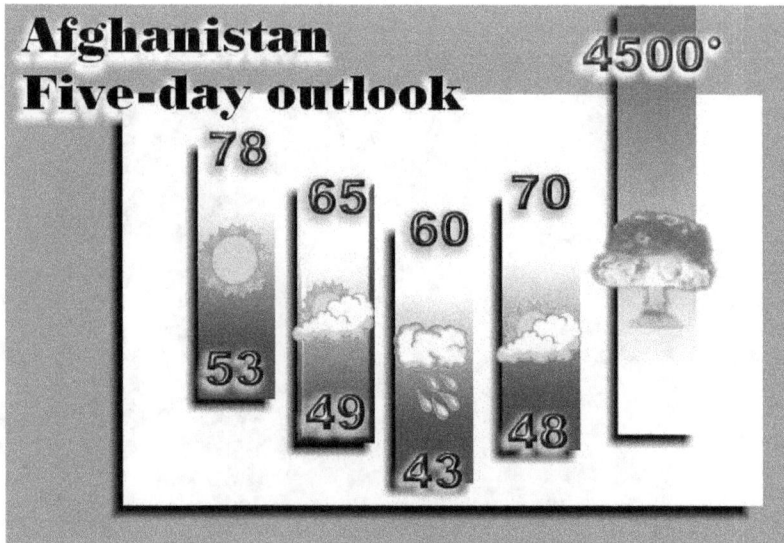

Foot Ball Cat

Redneck Swimming Pool

Positive proof of global warming.

Canada Border Patrol

CHAPTER 15 BEER AND LIQUOR AND BEVERAGES

GOT TO LOVE MINNESOTA

A Texan, a guy from Iowa, and a Minnesotan are riding horses out on the range.. The Texan, just to show off, pulls an expensive bottle of whiskey out of his saddlebag, takes a couple drinks, throws the bottle in the air, pulls out his gun and shoots it in mid-air. The guy from Iowa is shocked and asks, "What are you doing? That's a perfectly good bottle of whiskey! "The Texan replies, "In Texas, there's plenty of whiskey and bottles are cheap! "A little while later, not wanting to bed one, the guy from Iowa pulls out a bottle of champagne, takes a few sips, throws the bottle into the air, pulls out his gun and shoots it, just like the Texan. The guy from Minnesota can't believe it. "What are you doing? That was a very expensive bottle of champagne. With a wink to the Texan he says "In Des Moines, there's plenty of champagne and bottles are cheap." About 15 minutes later, the Minnesotan pulls out a bottle of beer. He opens it and takes a sip. Then another sip. Then he chugs the rest of the bottle. Then places the bottle back in his saddlebag, pulls out his gun and shoots the guy from Iowa. The Texan is visibly shaken. "What did you do that for?!? !"The Minnesotan replies, "Well, in Minnesota, we have plenty of people from Iowa, and bottles are returnable.

THIS PROVES ALCOHOL AND MUSIC DON'T MIX...

The orchestra conductor had been having problems with the bassists; they were the least professional of his musicians. It was the last performance of the season, Beethoven's 9th Symphony, which required extra effort from the bassists at the end. Earlier that evening, he had found them celebrating a birthday by passing around a bottle. Then, as he was about to cue the bassists, he knocked over his music stand. The sheet music scattered. So he stood in front of his orchestra, his worst fear realized: It was the bottom of the 9th, no score and the bassists were loaded.

HANGOVER RATING SYSTEM

One Star Hangover

No pain. No real feeling of illness. You're able to function relatively well. However, you are still parched. You can drink 5 sodas and still feel this way. For some reason, you are craving a steak & fries.

Two Star Hangover

No pain, but something is definitively amiss. You may look okay, but you have the mental capacity of a staple gun. The coffee you are chugging is only increasing your rumbling gut, which is still tossing around the fruity pancake from the 3:00 AM Waffle House excursion. There is some definite havoc being wreaked upon your bowels.

Three Star Hangover

Slight headache. Stomach feels crappy. You are definitely not productive.

Anytime a girl walks by you gag because her perfume reminds you of the flavored schnapps shots your alcoholic friends dared you to drink. Life would be better right now if you were home in your bed watching Lucy returns. You've had 4 cups of coffee, a gallon of water, 3 iced teas and a diet Coke yet you peed once.

Four Star Hangover

Life sucks. Your head is throbbing. You can't speak too quickly or else you might puke. Your boss has already lambasted you for being late and has given you a lecture for reeking of booze. You wore nice clothes, but you can't hide the fact that you only shaved one side of your face. (For the ladies, it looks like you put your make up on while riding the bumper cars).

Your eyes look like one big vein, and even your hair hurts. Your sphincter is in perpetual spasm, and the first of about five shots you take during the day brings water to the eyes of everyone who enters the bathroom.

Five Star Hangover

You have a second heartbeat in your head, which is actually annoying the employee who sits in the next cube. Vodka vapor is seeping out of every pore and making you dizzy. You still have toothpaste crust in the corners of your mouth from brushing your teeth in an attempt to get the remnants of the poop fairy out. Your body has lost the ability to generate saliva so your tongue is suffocating you. You don't have the foggiest idea who the hell the stranger was passed out in your bed this morning. Any attempt to defecate results in a fire hose like discharge of alcohol-scented fluid with a rare

"floater" thrown in . The sole purpose of this "floater" seems to be to splash the toilet water all over your ass. Death sounds pretty good about right now…

MONTANA BEAR

A bear walks into a bar in Billings, Montana and sits down. He bangs on the bar with his paw and demands a beer. The bartender approaches and says, "We don't serve beer to bears in bars in Billings."

The bear, becoming angry, demands again that he be served a beer.

The bartender tells him again, more forcefully, "We don't serve beer to belligerent bears in bars in Billings."

The bear, very angry now, says, "If you don't; serve me a beer, I'm going to eat that lady sitting at the end of the bar." The bartender says, "Sorry, we don't serve beer to belligerent, bully bears in bars in Billings."

The bear goes to the end of the bar, as promised, eats the woman. He comes back to his seat and again demands a beer. The bartender states, Sorry, we don't serve beer to belligerent, bully bears in bars in Billings who are on drugs." The bear says, "I'm NOT on drugs."

The bartender says, "You are now. That was a barbitchyouate."

SHIPMENT

An Airplane full of a shipment of Pepsi flying over Africa had malfunctioned, and went down. A few weeks later, Pepsi sent a rescue plane. They searched the area and found a tribe of cannibals. They walked up to the Chief of the tribe and asked him if he know anything about the crash. The Chief said, "Yeah. " When asked where the crew was, the Chief replied,

"We ate the crew, and we drank the Pepsi." The rescue crew were shocked. One man asked, "Did you eat their legs?" The Chief replied, "We at their legs, and we drank the Pepsi."

Another rescuer asked, "Did you eat their arms?" The Chief said, "We ate their arms, and we drank the Pepsi." After looking totally perplexed for a minute, a third asked, "Did you..you know..eat their ..ah ,err, 'things?" The Chief said, "No." "No?" asked the rescuers.

"No," replied the Chief, "Things go better with Coke."

THE SURVIVORS

Two guys of limited intelligence were on a ship that sand in the middle of the ocean.

They managed to inflate a rubber life raft and grab a box of provisions before their ship slipped below the surface. After floating under blazing heat for 6 days they ran out of food and water. On the 10th day, bleary-eyed and half dead from heat, thirst, and starvation. They spotted a small object floating toward them in the water. As it drew near, they were ecstatic to find that it was an oil lamp (the kind the genies come in). they grabbed the lamp and rubbed it. POOF!

Out popped a tired old genie who said, "OK, so you freed me from this stupid lamp, yadda yadda, yadda. But hey, I've been doing this three wishes stuff for a long time now and quite frankly I'm burned out. You guys get only ONE wish and then I'm outta here. Make it a good one." The first guy, without hesitation or thought, blurted out, "Give us all the beer we can drink for the rest of our lives!" "Fine," said the genie, and he instantly turned the entire ocean into beer and disappeared. "Great move Einstein!" said the second guy, slapping the first guy in the head.

"Now we're gonna have to piss in the boat!"

BEER DRINKING BAPTIST COWBOY

A cowboy walks into a bar in Texas, orders three mugs of brew andsits in the back room, drinking a sip out of each one in turn. When he finishes them, he comes back to the bar and orders three more. The bartender approaches and tells him, "You know, a mug goes flat after I draw it, so it would taste better if you bought just one at a time." The cowboy replies,

"Well, you see, I have two brothers. One is in Australia, the other is in Dublin and I'm in Texas. When we all left home, we promised that we'd drink this way to remember the days we were together. So I drink one for each of my brothers and one for myself." The bartender admits that this is a nice custom and leaves it there. The cowboy becomes a regular in the bar, and always drinks the same way. He orders three mugs and drinks them in turn.One day, he comes in and orders only two mugs! All the regulars take notice and fall silent. When he comes back to the bar for the second round, the bartender says, "I don't want to intrude on your grief, but I wanted to offer my condolences on your loss." The cowboy looks quite puzzled for a moment, then a light dawns and he laughs. "Oh, no, everybody's just fine,"he explains......."It's just that my wife and I joined the Baptist Church and obviously I had to quit drinking. Hasn't affected my brothers though."

WINES IN A RETAIL CHAIN

Some Wal-Mart customers will soon be able to sample new discount wine items.

Their own brand of wines affordable spirits at a price range of $2- $5. While wine connoisseurs may not be inclined to throw a bottle of Wal-Mart brand wine into their shopping carts, there is a market for cheap wine. The right name is important!

Here are a few suggested names:

1. Chateau traileur Parc
2. White Trashfindel
3. Big Red Gulp
4. Grape Expectations
5. Domaine Wal-Mart "Merde du Pays"
6. NASCARbernet
7. Chef Boyardeaux
8. Peanut Noir
9. Chateau due Moines
10. I Can't Belive It's Not Vinegar!

11. World championship Riesling

YOU HAVE HAD TOO MUCH COFFEE WHEN

Juan Valdez names his donkey after you.
You get a speeding ticket even when you're parked.
You grind your coffee beans in your mouth.
You sleep with your eyes open.
You watch videos in fast-forward.
You lick your coffeepot clean.
Your eyes stay open when you sneeze.
The nurse need scientific calculator to take your pulse.
You can watch videos in fast-forward.
You lick your coffeepot clean.
Your eyes stay open when you sneeze.
The nurse needs a scientific calculator to take your pulse.
You can type sixty words a minute with your feet.
You can jump-start your car without cables.
Your only source of nutrition comes from sweet & low.
You don't sweat, you percolate.
You've worn out the handle on your favorite coffee mug.
You go to AA meetings just for the free coffee.
You've worn the finish on your coffee table.
The Taster's choice couple wants to adopt you.
Starbucks own the mortgage on your house.
You're so wired you pick up FM radio.
Your life's goal is to "amount to a hill of beans."
Instant coffee takes too long.
You just want to be cremated just so you can spend eternity
in a coffee can.
You name yours cats Cream and Sugar.
Your lips are permanently stuck in the sipping position.
Your first-aid kit contains two pints of coffee with and I.V.
hookup.

BEER PRAYER

Our Lager,
Which art in barrels,
Hallowed be thy drink.
Thy will be drunk,
(I will be drunk),
At home as in the tavern.
Give us this day our foamy head,
And forgive us our spillages,
As we forgive those who spill against us.
And lead us not to incarceration,
But deliver us from hangovers.
For Thine is the beer,
The bitter and the lager.
Forever and ever,
Barmen.

ONE LINERS BAR

Two peanuts walk into a bar, and one was salted.

A sandwich walks into a bar and the bartender says, "Sorry we don't serve food in here."

A dyslexic man walks into a bra.

A man walks into a bar with a slab of asphalt under his arm and says, "A beer please, and one for the road."

CHAPTER 16 SEX

THE DATE

A man and a women were dating. She being of a religious nature had held back the worldly pleasure that he wanted from her so bad. In fact, he had never even seen her naked. One day, as they drove down the freeway, she remarked about his slow driving habits.

"I can't stand it anymore," she told him. "Let's play a game." "For every 5 miles per hour over the speed limit you drive, I'll remove one piece of clothing."

He enthusiastically agreed and sped up the car. He reached 55 MPH mark, so she took off her blouse. At 60 off came the pants. At 65 it was her bra and at 70 her panties.

Now seeing her naked for the first time and traveling faster than he ever had before, he became very excited and lost control of the car. He veered off the road, went over an embankment and hit a tree. His girlfriend not hurt but he was trapped.

She tried to pull him free but alas he as stuck.

"Go to the road and get help," he said. " I don't have anything to cover myself with!" she replied. The man felt around, but could only reach one of his shoes.

"You'll have to put this between your legs to cover it up," he told her.

So she did as he said and went up to the road for help. Along came a truck driver. Seeing a naked, crying women along the road, he pulled over to hear her story.

"My boyfriend! My boyfriend!" she sobs, "He's stuck and I can't pull him out!"

The truck driver looking down at the shoe between her legs replies, "Ma'am, if he's in that far, I'm afraid he's a goner!"

MATHEMATICS ONLY WORKS FOR THE YEAR 2002

This is pretty neat how it works out. This is cool math!!! It takes less than a minute.

DON'T CHEAT BY LOOKING AHEAD OR SCROLLING DOWN FIRST!

This is not one of those waste of time things, it is fun.

Work this out as you read. Be sure you don't read the bottom until you've worked it out!

1. First of all, pick the number of times a week that you would like to have SEX. (try for more than once but less then 10)

2. Multiply this number by 2 (Just to be bold)

3. Add 5 (for Sunday)

4. Multiply it by 50 . I'll wait while you get the calender.

5. If you have already had your birthday this year add 1752... If you haven't had your birthday this year add 1751

6. Now subtract the four digit year that you were born.

You should have a three digit number....

The first digit of this was your original number (i.e.,how many times you want to have SEX each week).

The next two numbers are.........

YOUR AGE! (Oh YES, it IS!!!!!)

SEXUAL POSITION

It has been determined that the most used sexual position for married couples is a doggie position. The husband sits up and begs.

The wife rolls over and plays dead.

THE THINGIE

There was a man who really took care of his body.

Lifted weights and jogged eight miles a day. One day, he

took a look in the mirror and noticed that he was tan all over accept for his "thingie."

So he decided to do something about it. He went to the beach, completely undressed himself and buried himself in the sand, except for his "thingie" which he left sticking up.

Two old ladies were strolling the beach, one using a cane. Upon seeing the "thingie"

sticking up over the sand, she began to move it around with her cane, remarking to the

other lady, "There's no justice in the world." The other lady asked what she meant.

She said, when I was 20, I was curious about it.

When I was 30, I enjoyed it.

When I was 40, I asked for it.

When I was 50, I paid for it.

When I was 60, I prayed for it.

When I was 70, I forgot about it.

Now, I am 80 and the damn things are growing wild on the beach and I'm too old to squat.

RECENT RESEARCH SHOWS THAT THERE ARE 5 KINDS OF SEX

The first kind of sex is Smurf Sex. This kind of sex happens when you first meet someone and you both have sex until you are blue in the face.

The second kind of sex is Kitchen Sex. This is when you have been with your partner for a short time and you are so horny you will have sex anywhere, even in the kitchen.

The third kind of sex is Bedroom Sex. This is when you have been with your partner for a long time. Your sex has gotten routine and you usually have sex in your bedroom.

The forth kind of sex is Hallway Sex. This is when you have been with your partner for too long. When you pass each other in the hallway you both say,

"Fuck You."

The fifth kind of sex is Courtroom Sex. This is when you cannot sand your partner any more and your partner takes you to court and screws you in front of everyone.

FLAT BELLY

A little boy walks into his parents' room to see his mom on top of his dad bouncing up and down. The mom sees her son and quickly dismounts, worried about what her son has seen. She dresses quickly and goes to find him.

The son sees his mom and asks, "What were you and Dad doing?"

The mother replies, "Well, you know your dad has a big tummy and sometimes I have to get on top of it and help flatten it." "You're wasting your time," said the boy.

"Why is that?" the mom asked puzzled. "Well when you go shopping the lady next door comes over and gets on her knees and blows it right back up."

Rental

A married businessman meets a beautiful girl and
agrees to spend the night with her for $500.
He spends the night with her but before he leaves,
He tells her that he does not have any cash with him,
But he will have his secretary write a check and mail it to her,
'RENT FOR APARTMENT.'
On the way to the office he regrets what he has done,
Realizing that the whole event was not worth the price.
So he has his secretary send a check for
$250 and enclosed the following typed note:
Dear Madam:

Enclosed you will find a check in the amount of $250 for rent of your Apartment. I am not sending the amount agreed upon, because when I Rented the apartment, I was under the impression that;

1) it had never been occupied;

2) that there was plenty of heat; and

3) that it was small enough to make me feel cozy and at home.

However, I found out that it had been previously occupied, That there wasn't any heat, and that it was entirely too large Upon receipt of the note,

The girl immediately returned the check for $250

With the following note:

Dear Sir,

First of all, I cannot understand how you expect a

Beautiful apartment to remain unoccupied indefinitely.

As for the heat, there is plenty of it,

If you know how to turn it on.

Regarding the space, the apartment is indeed of regular size, But if you don't have enough furniture to fill it,

Please don't blame the landlady.

Send the rent in full or we will be forced to

Contact your present landlady

CLUBS

Who is the most popular guy at the nudist colony?

The guy who can carry a cup of coffee in each hand and a dozen donuts.

BUNNIES

Why don't bunnies make noise when they have sex?

Because they have cotton balls.

AGE COUNTS

What does a 75 year old woman have between her breasts?
Her navel.

CONDOM SLOGANS

1. Cover your stump before you hump.
2. Before you attack her, wrap your whacker.
3. Dont's be silly, protect your willy.
4. When in doubt, shroud your spout.
5. Don't be loner, cover your boner.
6. You can't go wrong if you shield your dong.
7. If you're not going to sack it, go home and whack it.
8. If you think she's spunky, cover your monkey.
9. If you slip between her thighs, be sure to condomize.
10. It will be sweeter if you wrap your Peter.
11. She won't get sick if you wrap your dick.
12. If you go in heat, package your meat.
13. While you're undressing venus, dress up your penis.
14. When you take off her pants and blouse, zip up your trouser mouse.
15. Especially in December, gift wrap your member.
16. Never, never deck her with an unwrapped pecker.
17. Don't be a fool, vulcanize your tool.
18. The right selection will protect your erection.
19. Wrap it in foil before checking her oil.
20. A crank with armor will never harm her.
21. No glove, no love.

ASSICONS

We all know what those cute computer symbols called "emoticons", where
:) means a smile

:(means frown and sometimes represented by
:-) and :-(respectively.
Well, how about some "assicons"?
(_!_) a regular ass
(__!__) a fat ass
(!) a tight ass
(_*_) a sore ass
{_!_} a swishy ass
(_o_) as ass that's been around
(_X_) leave my ass alone
(_zzz_) a tired ass
(_o^^o_) a wise ass
(E=mc2) a smart ass
(_$_) money coming out of his ass
(_?_) dumb ass

```
           ' 'oo*'''''**oo.oo*'''*oo..
              oo*''           "''*o.o*''   "*o.
       .o''           'o''          "o
       o               o            *o
       o               o            'o
       o               o            o.
       o              \o/           o
       o             --O--          o
       o              /o\           o
       o.              o            o
       o               o            o
       oo              o            oo
       'ooo.          .oo.          ooo
       O ""oo,,    ,,oO'Oo,   ,,,,,oo"o    Big Ass
          o.          oo,           o
          'o          oo            o
           o           o            o
            o          o            o
             o         o            o
```

LOVE DRESS

The mother –in-law stopped by the married couple's house. She rang the door bell

And stepped into the house to see her daughter-in-law standing naked by the door.

"What are you doing?" the mother-in-law asked.

"I am waiting for my husband to come home from work," the daughter-in-law replied.

"Why are you naked?" asked the mother-in-law.

"This is my Love dress," the daughter-in-law replied. "Love dress!" you are naked," said the mother-in-law. "But my husband loves it when I wear this dress. It makes him happy and makes me happy," said the daughter-in-law, "I would appreciate your leaving now because my husband will be home any minute," the daughter-in-law continued.

Tired of all of this romantic stuff, the mother-in –law left. On the way home, she thought about the "Love Dress" and got an idea. She undressed, showered, applied her best perfume, and waited by the door for her husband to come home.

Finally, the pickup truck drove up the driveway, and waited by the boor for her husband to come home. Finally, the pickup truck drove up the driveway, and she took her place by the door. The father-in-law opened the door, and immediately saw his wife naked by the door. "What are you doing?" he asked. "This is my love dress, "the mother-in-law replied. "Needs ironing," he replied.

THE RAISE

The penis, hereby requests a raise in salary for the following reasons:

I do physical labor .

I work at great depths.

I work head first.

I don to get weekends off or public holidays.

I work in a damp environment.

I don't get paid overtime or shift penalties.

I work in a dark workplace that has poor ventilation.

I work in high temperatures.

My work exposes me to contagious diseases.

Response from the Management

After assessing your request, and considering the arguments you have raised, the administration rejects your request for the following reasons:

You do not work 8 hours straight.

You fall asleep on the job after brief work periods.

You do not always follow the orders of the management team.

You do not stay in your allocated position, and often visit other areas.

You do not take initiative, you need to be pressured and stimulated in order to start working.

You leave the workplace rather messy at the end of your shift.

You don't always observe safety measures, such as wearing the correct protective outfits.

You don't wait till pension age before retiring.

You don't like working double shifts.

You sometimes leave your allocated position before you have completed the day's work.

And if that were not all, you have been seen constantly entering and leaving the work place carrying 2 suspicious looking bags.

KING ARTHUR'S COURT

King Arthur was worried about leaving Queen Guinevere alone with all those horny knights of the Round Table. So he went to Merlin for some advice.

After explaining his predicament to Merlin, the wizard looked thoughtful, and said

That he'd see if he could come up with something, and asked him to come back in a week. A week later King Arthur was back in Merlin's laboratory where the good wizard was showing him his latest invention. It was a chastity belt ... except that it had a rather large hole in the most obvious place. "This is no good, Merlin!" the king exclaimed,

"Look at this opening. How is this supposed to protect m'lady, the Queen?"

"Ah, sire, just observe." Said Merlin as he searched his cluttered work bench until he found what he was looking for. He then selected his most worn-out wands, one that he was going to discard anyway. He then inserted it in the gaping aperture of the chastity belt where upon a small guillotine blade came down and cut it neatly in two.

"Merlin, you are a genius!" said the grateful monarch, "Now I can leave, knowing that my Queen if fully protected." After putting Guinevere in the device, King Arthur then set out upon his Quest. Several years passed until he returned to Camelot. Immediately he assembled all his knights in the courtyard and had them drop their trousers for an informal "short arm" inspection. Sure enough! Each and every one of them was either amputated or mutilated in some way... All of them except Sir Galahad.

"Sir Galahad," exclaimed King Arthur, "The one and only true knight!" "Only you among all the nobles have been true to me. What is it in my power to grant you?"

"Name it and it is yours!"

But sir Galahad was speechless….

OLD DILAPIDATED BOAT

Joe and John were identical twins. Joe owned an old dilapidated boat and kept pretty much to himself. One day the rented out his boat to a group of out-of-staters who ended up sinking it. He spent all day trying to salvage as much stuff as he could from the sunken vessel and was out of touch all that day and most of the evening. Unbeknownst to him, his brother John's wife had died suddenly in his absence.

When he got back on shore he went into town to pick up a few things at the grocery. A kind old woman there mistook him for John and said, "I'm so sorry for your loss. You must feel terrible." Joe, thinking she was talking about his boat said, "Hell no! Fact is I'm sort of glad to be rid of her. She was a rotten old thing from the beginning. Her bottom was all shriveled up and she smelled like old dead fish. She was always holding water. She had a bad crack in the back and pretty big hole in the front too. Every time I used her, her hole got bigger and she leaked like crazy." "I guess what finally finished her off was when I rented her to those four guys looking for a good time. I warned them that she wasn't very good and that she smelled bad. But they wanted her anyway. The damn fools tried to get in her all at one time and she split right up the middle."

The old woman fainted.

BARBERSHOP

A little girl goes to the barber shop with her father. She stands next to the barber chair, eating a snake cake while her dad gets he hair cut. The barber smiles at her and says, "sweetheart, you're going to get hair on your Twinkie." "I know," she replies. " I'm gonna get tits too."

COMPUTER CONSULTANT

A female computer consultant was helping a smug male set up his computer and asked him what word he would like to use as a password to log in with.

Wanting to embarrass the female he told her to enter "PENIS".

Without blinking or saying a word she entered the password.

The computers response: Password Rejected. Not Long Enough.

CHAMPAGNE

A man enters a restaurant and while sitting at his table, notices a gorgeous woman sitting at another table, alone. He calls the waiter over and sasks for the most expensive bottle of champagne to be sent over to her, knowing if she accepts it, she is his. The waiter gets the bottle and quickly sends it over to the girl, saying this sis from the gentleman. She looks at the champagne and decides to send a note with the bottle back over to the man.

The note read: "For me to accept this bottle, you need to have a Mercedes in your garage,

$1M in the bank , and 7 inches in your pants." Well, the man, after reading this note, sends one of his own back to her and it reads: "Just so you know, I happen to have 2 Mercedes in the garage, I have over $2M in the bank, but not even for YOU, would I cut off 2 inches! Send the bottle back.

WE REGRET TO INFORM YOU

It was with great sorrow that I have to inform that the world was stunned by the news of the death of the energizer bunny. He was 18 years old. Authorities believe that the death occurred at approximately 8:42 last evening. Best known as the irritating pink bunny that just kept going and going. Pinkie, as his friends called him, was alone at the time of his death. An emergency autopsy was performed early this morning by Chief Medical Examiner, Dura Cell. He concluded that cause of death was acute cardiac arrest, induced by sexual overstimulation. Apparently someone had put the bunny's batteries in backwards and he kept coming and coming and coming.

FATHEAD

A man and his son walk into an ice cream parlor. The man orders two vanilla cones, looks at his son, slaps him on the back of the head and says "What do you want, Fathead?" The guy at the counter was appalled. He asked the man why he did that. The man said "There are three things a man wants in life, 1)A Big truck. You see that truck out there, biggest damn truck in the county. 2)A nice house. I got the nicest house in the state. And 3) a tight pussy. And I had me one of them until fathead here came along.

ARTIFICIAL INSEMINATION

A man buys several sheep, hoping to breed them for wool. After several weeks, he notices that none of the sheep are getting pregnant, and calls a vet for help. The vet tells him that he should try artificial insemination. The guy doesn't have the slightest idea what this means. Not wanting to display his ignorance, only asks the vet how he will know when the sheep are pregnant. The vet tells him that they will stop standing around and will, instead, lie down and wallow in the grass when they are pregnant. The man hangs up and gives it some thought. He comes to the conclusion that artificial insemination means he has to impregnate the sheep. So, he loads the sheep into his truck, drives them out into the woods, has sex with them all, brings them back and goes to bed.

Next morning, he wakes and looks out at the sheep. Seeing that they are all still standing around, he concludes that the first try didn't take, and loads them in the truck again. He drives them out to the woods, bangs each sheep twice for good measure, brings them back and goes to bed. Next morning, he wakes to find the sheep still just standing around.

One more try, he tells himself, and proceeds to load them up and drive them out to the woods. He spends all day shagging the sheep and, upon returning home, falls listlessly into bed. The next morning, he cannot even raise himself from the bed to look at the sheep. He asks his wife to look out and tell him if the sheep are lying in the grass. "No," she says, "they're all in the truck and one of them is honking the horn."

PUMPKIN PATCH

In summary, the police arrested Patrick Lawrence, a 22-year old white male, resident of Dacula, GA, in a pumpkin patch at 11:38 p.m. on Friday. Lawrence will be charged with lewd and lascivious behavior, public indecency, and public intoxication at the Gwinnett County courthouse on Monday. The suspect explained that as he was passing a pumpkin patch he decided to stop. "You know, a pumpkin is soft and squishy inside, and there was no one around here for miles. At least I thought there wasn't," he stated in a phone interview. Lawrence went on to say that he pulled over to the side of the road, picked out a pumpkin that he felt was appropriate to his purposes, cut a hole in it, and proceeded to satisfy his alleged," "need." "I guess I was just really into it, you know?" he commented with evident embarrassment. In the process, Lawrence apparently failed to notice a Gwinnett County police car approaching and was unaware of his audience until officer

Brenda Taylor approached him. "It was an unusual situation, that's for sure," said Officer Taylor. "I walked up to (Lawrence) and he's … just working away at his pumpkin."Taylor went on to describe what happened when she approached Lawrence. "I just went up and said, "Excuse me sir, but do you realize that you are screwing pumpkin?" He froze and was clearly very surprised that I was there, and then looked me straight in the face and said, "A pumpkin? Damn… is it midnight already?"

THE PET

A woman went into the pet shop to buy her husband a pet. After looking around she realized that all the pets there were very expensive. She went to the counter and questioned the clerk. 'I wanted to buy my husband a pet, but all of your are so expensive," she said. "Well," said the clerk, "I have a huge bullfrog in the back for $50.00? Would you like to see it?" "$50.00? For a frog?" asked the woman. The clerk said, "It's a special frog. It gives blow jobs." Well, the woman did not particularly enjoy giving head, so, she thought this was a heck of a deal. She'd get her husband a gift he'd surely enjoy, and she'd never have to do that again. The woman decided to buy the frog. She took it home to her husband and explained the strange gift. Of course, the husband was a bit skeptical, but said for sure he'd try it out that night. The woman went to bed that night relieved knowing she'd never have to give another blow job. Around two in the morning, she woke up to hearing pots and pans banging around in the kitchen. She got up to see what was going on. When she got to the kitchen she saw her husband and the frog, sitting at the kitchen table like best buddies, looking through cook books. "What are you tow doing looking through cook books at this hour?" asked the woman. The guy looks up at her and says, "Well, if I can teach this frog to cook, your ass is outta here!"

SEX ONE LINERS

What do you say to a virgin when she sneezes? Goes-in-tight.

What does a 72 year olds snatch taste like? Depends.

What's "68"? You do me and I owe you one.

What did Cinderella do when she got to the ball? Gagged.

What do you call a man who cries while he masturbates? A tearjerker.

How many perverts does it take to put in a light bulb? Just one, but it takes the entire emergency room to get it out.

What's the definition of a teenager? God's punishment for enjoying sex.

What's the definition of a vagina? The box a penis comes in.

What two works will clear out a men's restroom? "Nice dick!"

What do you call kinky sex with chocolate? S&M&M.

Define transvestite: A guy who likes to eat, drink, and be Mary.

What do a dildo and soy beans have in common? They are both used as substitute meat.

What do you call kids born in a whorehouses? Brothel sprouts.

What is every Amish woman's private fantasy? Two Mennonite.

What did the cannibal get when he was late for dinner? The cold shoulder.

What do you call a smiling Roman with pubic hair between his teeth? Gladiator.

How do you make 5 lbs. look good? Put a nipple on it.

What should you do if your girlfriend starts smoking? Slow down and use a better lubricant.

If Eve wore a fig leaf, what did Adam wear? A hole in it.

5 KINDS OF SEX

Smurf sex- This happens during the honeymoon, you both keep doing it until you're blue in the face.

Kitchen sex- This is at the beginning of the marriage, you'll have sex anywhere, anytime, even in the kitchen.

Bedroom Sex- You're calmed down a bit, perhaps have kids, so you gotta do it in the bedroom.

Hallway Sex- This is where you pass each other in the hallway and say "Fuck You!"

Courtroom Sex- This is when you get divorced and your wife screws you in front of everyone in the courtroom.

CHAPTER 17 MISCELLANEOUS

THE SENDER

There was a person who sent ten different puns to his friends, with hope that at least one of the puns would make them laugh. Unfortunately, no pun in ten did.

POLITICS MEASURED IN COWS

DEMOCRAT You have two cows. Your neighbor has none. You feel guilty for being successful. Barbara Streisand sings at your birthday party. REPUBLICAN You have two cows. Your neighbor has none. So? SOCIALIST You have two cows. The government takes one and gives it to your neighbor. You form a cooperative to tell him how to manage his cow. COMMUNIST You have two cows. The government seizes both and provides you with milk.. You wait in line for hours to get it. It is expensive and sour. CAPITALISM, AMERICAN STYLE You have two cows. You sell one, buy a bull, and build a herd of cows. DEMOCRACY, AMERICAN STYLE You have two cows. The government taxes you to the point you have to sell both to support a man in a foreign country who has only one cow, which was a gift from your government.

BUREAUCRACY AMERICAN STYLE

You have two cows. The government takes them both, shoots one, milks the other, pays you for the milk, and then pours the milk down the drain. AMERICAN CORPORATION You have two cows. You sell one, lease it back to yourself and do an IPO on the 2nd one. You force the two cows to produce the milk of four cows. You are surprised when one cow drops dead. You spin an announcement to the analysts stating you have downsized and are reducing expenses. Your stock goes up. FRENCH CORPORATION You have two cows. You go on strike because you want three cows. You go to lunch and drink wine. Life is good. JAPANESE CORPORATION You have two cows. You redesign them so they are one-tenth the size of an ordinary cow and produce twenty times the milk. They learn to travel on unbelievably crowded trains. Most are at the top of their class at cow school. GERMAN CORPORATION You have two cows. You engineer them so they are all blond, drink lots of beer, give excellent quality milk, and run a hundred miles an hour. Unfortunately they also demand 13 weeks of vacation per year. ITALIAN CORPORATION You have two cows but you don't know where they are. While ambling around, you see a beautiful woman. You break for lunch. Life is good.

RUSSIAN CORPORATION

You have two cows. You have some vodka. You count them and learn you have five cows. You have some more vodka. You count them again and learn you have 42 cows. The Mafia shows up and takes over however many cows you really have. TALIBAN CORPORATION You have all the cows in Afghanistan, which are two. You don't milk them because you cannot touch any creature's private parts. Then you kill them and claim a US bomb blew them up while they were in the hospital. IRAQI CORPORATION You have two cows. They go in hiding. They send radio tapes of their mooing. POLISH CORPORATION You have two bulls. Employees are regularly maimed and killed attempting to milk them. FLORIDA CORPORATION You have a black cow and a brown cow. Everyone votes for the best looking one. Some of the people who like the brown one best, vote for the black one. Some people vote for both. Some people vote for neither. Some people can't figure out how to vote at all. Finally, a bunch of guys from out-of-state tell you which is the best-looking cow. CALIFORNIA CORPORATION You have millions of cows. Most are illegals. Arnold likes the ones with the big tits.

DATELINE NEW YORK CITY

At New York's Kennedy airport today, an individual later discovered to be a public school teacher was arrested trying to board a flight while in possession of a ruler, a protractor, a setsquare, a slide rule, and a calculator. At a morning press conference, Attorney general John Ashcroft said he believes the man is a member of the notorious al-gebra movement. He is being charged by the FBI with carrying weapons of math instruction "Al-gebra is a fearsome cult," Ashcroft said. "They desire average solutions by means and extremes, and sometimes go off on tangents in a search of absolute value. They use secret code names like "x" and "y" and refer to themselves as "unknowns", but we have determined they belong to a common denominator of the axis of medieval with coordinates in every country."As the Greek philanderer Isosceles used to say, there are 3 sides to every triangle," Ashcroft declared. When asked to comment on the arrest, President Bush said, "If God had wanted us to have better weapons of math instruction, He would have given us more fingers and toes."I am gratified that our government has given us a sine that it is intent on protracting us from these math-dogs who are willing to disintegrate us with calculus disregard. Murky statisticians love to inflict plane on every sphere of influence," the President said, adding: "Under the circumferences, we must differentiate their root, make our point, and draw the line."President Bush warned, "These weapons of math instruction have the potential to decimal everything in their math on a scalene never before seen unless we become exponents of a Higher Power and begin to factor-in random facts of vertex."Attorney General Ashcroft said, "As our Great Leader would say, read my ellipse. Here is one principle he is uncertainty of: though they continue to multiply, their days are numbered as the hypotenuse tightens around their necks."You can't be too careful with all these radicals.

FRENCH ONE LINER PUN
Don't Scarf the French Fries
We Scarf our American Fries down.

AN OFFICE MANAGER GIVEN THE TASK OF HIRING AN INDIVIDUAL TO FILL A JOB OPENING.
After sorting through a stack of resumes he found
Four people who were equally qualified.
He decided to call the four in and ask them only one question. Their answer would determine which of them would get the job.

The day came and as the four sat around the conference room table the interviewer asked, "What is the fastest thing you know of?"

Acknowledging the first man on his right, the man replied, "A THOUGHT. It just pops into your head. There's no warning that it's on the way; it's just there. A thought is the fastest thing I know of."

"That's very good!" replied the interviewer. "And now you sir?" he asked the second man.

"Hmm....let me see. A blink! It comes and goes and you don' t know that it ever happened. A BLINK is the fastest thing I know of."

"Excellent!" said the interviewer. "The blink of an eye... that's a very popular cliché for speed."

He then turned to the third man who was contemplating his reply.

"Well, out at my dad's ranch, you step out of the house and on the wall there's a light switch. When you flip that switch, way out across the pasture the light in the barn comes on in less than an instant. Yep, TURNING ON A LIGHT is the fastest thing I can think of."

The interviewer was very impressed with the third answer and thought he had found his man. "It's hard to beat the speed of light" he said.

Turning to the fourth and final man, the interviewer posed the same question The last man replied, "After hearing the three previous answers, It's obvious to me that the fastest thing known is DIARRHEA."

"WHAT!?" said the interviewer, stunned by the response.

"Oh I can explain." said the fourth man. "You see the other day I wasn't feeling so good and I ran for the bathroom. But, before I could

THINK, BLINK, or TURN ON THE LIGHT, I had already shit my pants!"

HE GOT THE JOB

LEMON SQUEEZE

The local bar was so sure that its bartender was the strongest man around that they offered a standing $1000 bet. The bartender would squeeze a lemon until all the juice ran into a glass, and hand the lemon to a patron. Anyone who could squeeze one more drop of juice out would win the money. Many people had tried over time -weightlifters, longshoremen, etc. But nobody could do it. One day a scrawny little man came in wearing thick glasses and a polyester suit, and said in a tiny, squeaky voice, "I'd like to try the bet." After the laughter had died down, the bartender said "okay", grabbed a lemon, and squeezed away. He then handed the wrinkled remains of the rind to the little man. But the crowd's laughter turned to total silence as the man clenched his fist around the lemon and six more drops of juice fell into the glass. As the crowd cheered, the bartender paid him the $1000, and asked the little man, "What do you do for a living? Are you a lumberjack, a weight lifter, or what?" "No", the man replied, "I work for the IRS."

COOL OFF

Three Goldberg brothers, Norman, Hyman, and Max invented and developed the first automobile air-conditioner.

On July 17th, 1946, when the temperature in Detroit was 97°, the 3 brothers walked into old man Henry Ford's office and sweet-talked his secretary into telling him that 3 gentlemen were there with the most exciting innovation in the auto industry since the electric starter.

Henry, curious, invited them into his office.

They refused and instead asked that he come out to the parking lot to their car. They persuaded him to get into the car -- which was about 130° -- turned on the air-conditioner and cooled the car off immediately.

The old man got very excited, invited them back to the office and offered them $3 million for the patent.

The brothers refused saying they would settle for $2 million but they wanted recognition by having a prominent label, "The Goldberg Air-Conditioner" on each car's dashboard at installation.

Now, old man Ford was more than just a little bit anti-Semitic. There was no way he would put the Goldbergs' name on two million Ford automobiles.

They haggled back and forth for about 2 hours, and finally agreed on $4 million, and that just their first names would be shown.

And so, even today, all Ford air-conditioners show, on the controls, their names "Norm, Hi, & Max."

AMERICAN IMMIGRANT

A Russian arrives in New York City as a new immigrant to the United States . He stops the first person he sees walking down the stre et and says, "Thank you Mr. American for letting me into this country, giving me housing, food stamps, free medical care, and a free education!" The passerby says, "You are mistaken, I am a Mexican." The man goes on and encounters another passerby. "Thank you for having such a beautiful country here in America ." The person says, "I not American, I Vietnamese." The new arrival walks farther, and the next person he sees he stops, shakes his hand, and says, "Thank you for wonderful America!" That person puts up his hand and says, "I am from Middle East . I am not American." He finally sees a nice lady and asks, "Are you an American?" She says, "No, I am from Africa ." Puzzled, he asks her, "Where are all the Americans?" The African lady checks her watch and says, "Probably at work."

LONE RANGER

The Lone Ranger and Tonto went camping in the desert. After they got to their tent all set up, they fell sound asleep.

Some hours later, the Lone Ranger wakes his faithful friend and says,

"Tonto, look up at the sky and tell me what you see?" Tonto replies, "Me see millions of stars."

"What does that tell you?" asked The Lone Ranger. Tonto ponders for a minute, then says,

"Astronomically speaking, it tells me that their millions of galaxies and potentially billions of planets. Astrologically, it tells me that Saturn is in Leo. Time wise, it appears to be approximately a quarter past three in the morning. Theologically, it's evident the Lord is all powerful and we are small and insignificant. Meteorologically, it seems we will have a beautiful day tomorrow.

What it tell you Kemo Sabi?" The Lone Ranger is silent for a moment, then says,

"Tonto, you do ass, someone has stolen are tent."

SERVICE

At one time I thought I had a handle on the word "service." Service being the act of doing things for other people. Then I heard of the terms:

Internal revenue Service
Postal Service
Civil Service
Service Stations
Customer Service
City/County Public Service
And I became confused about the word "service".

EXERCISE FOR PEOPLE 50 AND OLDER

Begin by standing on a comfortable surface, where you have plenty of room at each side. With a 5-lb potato bag in each hand, extend your arms straight out from your sides and hold them there as long as you can.

Try to reach a full minute, and then relax. Each day, you'll find that you can hold this position for just a bit longer.

After a couple of weeks, move up to 10-lb potato bags. Then try 50-lb potato bags and then eventually try to get to where you can lift a 100-lb potato bag in each hand and hold your arms straight for more than a full minute. (I'm at this level.)

After you feel confident at that level, put a potato in each bag.

YARD WORK

A man is doing yard work and his wife is about to take a shower. The man realizes that he can't find the rake. He yells up to his wife, to look out the window and says "Where is the rake?"

Whe can't hear him and shouts back, "What?" The man first points to his eye, then points to his knee and finally makes a raking motion. The wife not sure and says, "What?" The man repeats his gestures,.. points to his eye, then point to his knee.. finally makes a raking motion. "Eye knee the rake" The wife understands and signals back. She first points to her eye… then she points to her butt… and finally to her crotch. Well, there is no way in hell the man can even come close to understanding that one. Exasperated, he goes upstairs and asks her "What the friggin ' hell was that?" She replies, Eye-Left Tit-Behind- The Bush.

I REGRET TO INFORM YOU LETTER

Dear Hiring Manager,

Thank you for your letter of March 16. After careful consideration, I regret to inform you that I am unable to accept your refusal to offer me a position in your company at this time.

This year I have been particularly fortunate in receiving an unusually large number of rejection letters. With such a varied and promising field of candidates, It is impossible for me to accept all refusals.

Despite your companies; outstanding qualifications and previous experience in rejecting applicants, I find that your rejection does not meet my needs at this time.

Therefore, I will assume the position in your department his August.

I look forward to seeing you then.

Best of luck in rejecting future applicants.

Sincerely,

Interviewee

ANAGRAM

As you know an Anagram is a word or a phrase made by trans- positioning, or rearranging the letters of another word or phrase. The following are exceptionally clever.

George Bush: When you rearrange the letters: He bugs Gore

Dormitory: whe you rearrange the letters: Dirty Room

Evangelist: When you rearrange the letters: Evil's Agent

Desperation: when you rearrange the letters: A Rope Ends It

The Morse Code: When you rearrange the letters: Here Comes Dots. Slot Machines: When you rearrange the letters: Cash Lost in 'em

Animosity: When you rearrange the letters: Is No Amity

Mother-in-law: When you rearrange the letters: Woman Hitler

Snooze Alarms: When you rearrange the letters: Alas! No More Z's

A Decimal Point: When you rearrange the letters: I'm A Dot In Place

The Earthquakes: When you rearrange the letters: That Queer Shake

Eleven plus two: When you rearrange the letters: Twelve plus one

President Clinton of the USA: It can be rearranged into: To Copulate He Finds Interns

SUNG TO THE TUNE OF THE BEVERLY HILLBILLIES THEME SONG

Come and listen to my story 'bout a boy name Bush.
His IQ was zero and his head was up his tush.
He drank like fish while he drove all about.
But that didn't matter 'cuz his daddy bailed him out.
DUI, that is, Criminal record. Cover-up

Well, the first thing you know little Georgie goes to Yale.
He can't spell his name but they never let him fail.
He spends all his time hangin' out with student folk.
And that's when he learns how to snort a line of coke.
Blow, that is, White gold. Nose candy.

The next thing you know there's a war in Vietnam.
Kin folks say, "George, stay at home with Mom."
Let the common people get maimed and scarred.
We'll buy you a spot in the Texas Air Guard.
Cushy, that is. Country clubs. Nose candy.

Twenty years later George gets a little bored.
He trades in the booze, says that Jesus is he Lord.

He said, "Now the White House is the place I wanna be."
So he called his daddy's friends and they called the GOP.
Gun owners, that is, Falwell. Jesse Helms.

Come November 7, the election ran late.
Kin folks say "Geb, give the boy your state!"
"Don't let those colored folks get into the polls."
So they put up barricades so they couldn't punch their holes.
Chads, that is. Duval County, Miami-Dade.

Before the votes were counted five Supremes stepped in .
Told all the voters "Hey, we want George to win."
"Stop counting votes!" was their solemn invocation.
And that's how George finally got his coronation.
Rigged, that is. Illegitimate, No moral authority.
Y'all come vote now. Obama Ya hear?

POLITICS EXPLAINED

A little boy goes to his Dad and asks, "What is politics?"
Dad says. "Well, son let me try to explain to you this way..

I'm the breadwinner of the family, so let's call me 'Capitalism.'

Your Mom, she;s the administrator of the household, so we'll call her the Government. We're here to take care you YOUR needs, so we'll call you 'The People.' The nanny, well, she works hard all day for very little money,

So we'll consider her 'The Working Class.' And your baby brother.. we'll call him 'The Future.' Now, think about that and see if it makes sense. So the little boy goes off to bed thinking about what his Dad has said. Later that night, he hears his baby brother crying, so he gets up to check on him. He finds that the baby has severely soiled his diaper. So the little boy goes to his parents' room and finds his mother sound asleep. Not wanting to wake her, he goes to the nanny's room. Finding the door locked he peeks into the keyhole and sees his father in bed with the nanny. He gives up and goes back to bed. The next morning, the little boy says to his father, "Dad, I think I understand the concept of politics now." The father says, "Good son, tell me in your own words what you think politics is all about." The little boy replies, "Well, whileCapitalism is screwing the Working Class, the Government is sound asleep, The People are being Ignored, and the Future is in deep shit.

VOTER ELECTION REQUEST

Due to an anticipated voter turnout much larger than originally expected, the polling facilities may not be able to handle the load all at once. Therefore, Republicans are requested to vote on Tuesday, November 7, and Democrats on Wednesday, November 8. Please pass this message along and help us to make sure that nobody gets left out.

DOUGHBOY

It is with the saddest heart that I have to pass on the following:

The Pillsbury Doughboy died Monday of sever yeast infection and complications from

Repeated pokes to the belly. He was 71.

Doughboy was buried in a lightly greased coffin.

Dozens of celebrities turned out, including Mrs. Butterworth, the California Raisins, Hungry

Jack, Betty Crocker, the Hostess Twinkies, and Captain Crunch. The grave side was piled high

With flours as long time friend Aunt Jemima delivered the eulogy, describing Doughboy as a man who "Never know how much he was kneaded." Doughboy rose quickly in show business but his later Life was filled with many turnovers. He was not considered a very smart cookie, wasting much of his dough on half-baked schemes. Despite being a little flaky at times, even as acrusty old man, he was considered a roll model for millions. Toward the end it was thought he'drise once again, but he was no tart. Doughboy is survived by his second wife, Play Dough. They have two children, and one in the oven. The funeral was held at 3:50 for about 20 minutes.

THE LAMP

A white guy is walking along a beach when he comes across a lamp partially buried in the sand.

He pick up the lamp and gives it a rub. Two genies appear and tell him he has been granted three wishes. The guy makes his three wished and the genies disappear. The next thing the guy knows, he's in a bedroom in a mansion surrounded by fifty beautiful women. He makes love to all of them and begins to explore the house. Suddenly, he feels something soft under his feet.

He looks down and the floor is covered with $100 bills. Then there's a knock at the door and standing there are two people dressed in Ku Klux Klan outfits. They drag him outside to the nearest tree, throw a rope over a limb and hang him by the neck until he is dead. The Klansmen walk off. As they are walking away they remove their hoods. It's the two genies. One genie says to the other one, "Hey, I can understand the first wish of having all these beautiful women in a big mansion to make love to, I can also understand wanting to be a millionaire. But to be hung like a black man is beyond me!

DELIVERY

The concierge tells him he's in luck, there's a pizza place that just opened, and they deliver. The concierge gives the business man the phone number, and he goes back to his room and orders a pizza. Thirty minutes later, the delivery guy shows up to the door with the pizza. The businessman takes the pizza, and starts sneezing uncontrollably. He asks the delivery man,

"What the heck did you put on this pizza?" the delivery man bows deeply and says, "We put on the pizza what you ordered, pepper only."

POLICE PULLOVER

A driver is pulled over by a police car one afternoon, and when the officer comes up to the window he asks, "Do you know why I pulled you over?" The driver responds, "No officer I don't."

The officer replies, "you ran that stop sign back there." "Well I slowed down to see if anyone was coming." responded the driver. "Step out of the car sir" As soon as the driver stepped out

The officer began to hit him with a knight stick. "Do you want me to stop or just slow down?"

TRAFFIC SCHOOL EXAM STUDENTS ANSWERS

What is the difference between a flashing red traffic light and a flashing yellow traffic light? The color.

Who has the right of way when four cars approach a four-way stop at the same time? The pick up truck with the gun rack and the bumper sticker saying, "Guns don't kill people . I do."

How can you reduce the possibility of having an accident? Be too drunk to find your keys.

What problems would you face if you were arrested for drunk driving? I'd probably lose my buzz a lot faster.

What changes would occur in your lifestyle if you could no longer drive lawfully? I would be forced to drive unlawfully.

What can you do to help ease a heavy traffic problem? Carry loaded weapons.

When driving through fog, what should you use? Your car.

GOVERNMENTS

Feudalism:

You have two cows. Your lord takes some of the milk.

Pure Socialism:

You have two cows. The government takes them and puts them in a barn with everyone else's cows. You have to take care of all the cows. The government gives you a glass of milk.

Bureaucratic Socialism:

Your cows are cared for by ex-chicken farmers. The government gives you as much milk and eggs the regulations say you should need.

Fascism:

You have two cows. The government takes both, hires you to take care of them, and sells you the milk.

Pure Communism:

You share two cows with your neighbors. You and your neighbors bicker about who has the most "ability" and who has the most "need". Meanwhile, no one works, no one gets any milk, and the cows drop dead of starvation.

Russian Communism:

You have two cows. You have to take care of them, but the government takes all the milk. You steal back as much milk as you can and sell it on the black market .

Perestroika:
You have two cows. You have to take care of them, but the Mafia takes all milk. You steal back as much milk as you can and sell it on the "free market".
Cambodian Communism:
You have two cows. The government takes both and shoots you.
Dictatorship:
You have two cows. The government takes both and drafts you.
Pure Democracy:
You have two cows. Your neighbors decide who gets the milk.
Representative Democracy:
You have two cows. Your neighbors pick someone to tell you who gets the milk.
Bureaucracy:
You have two cows. At first the government regulates what you can feed them and when you can milk them. Then it pays you not to milk them. Then it takes both, shoots one, milks the other and pours the milk down the drain. Then it requires you to fill out forms accounting for the missing cows.
Capitalism:
You don't have any cows. The bank will not lend you money to buy cows, because you don't have any cows to put up as collateral.
Pure Anarchy:
You have two cows. Either you sell the milk at a fair price or your neighbors try to take the cows and kill you.
Anarcho-Capitalism:
You have two cows. You sell one and buy a bull.
Surrealism:
You have two giraffes. The government requires you to take harmonica lessons.

THREE LIFE LESSONS

Lesson Number One

A crow was sitting on a tree, doing nothing all day. A small rabbit saw the crow, and asked him,

"Can I also sit like you and do nothing all day long?"

The crow answered: "Sure, why not." So, the rabbit sat on the ground below the crow, and reasted. All of a sudden, a fox appeared, jumped on the rabbit and ate it.

Moral of the story is : To be sitting and doing nothing, you must be sitting very, very high up.

Lesson Number Two

A turkey was chatting with a bull. "I would love to be able to get to the top of that tree," sighed

The turkey, "but I haven't got the energy."

"Well, why don't you nibble on some of my droppings?" replied the bull. "They're packed with nutrients. The turkey pecked at a lump of dung and found that it actually gave him enough strength to reach the first branch of the tree. The next day. After eating some more dung, he reached the second branch. Finally after a fortnight, there he was proudly perched at the top of the tree. Soon he was promptly spotted by a farmer, who shot the turkey out of the tree. Moral of the story: Bullshit might get you to the top, but it won't keep you there.

Lesson Number Three

A little bird was flying south for the winter. It was so cold, the bird froze and fell to the ground in a large field. While it was lying there, a cow came by and dropped some dung on it. As the frozen bird lay there in the pile of cow dung, it began to realize how warm it was. The dung was actually thawing him out! He lay there all warm and happy, and soon began to sing for joy.

A passing cat heard the bird singing and came to investigate. Following the sound, the cat discovered the bird under the pile of cow dung. And promptly dug him out and ate him!

The morals of the story are:
1)Not everyone who drops shit on you is your enemy.
2)Not everyone who gets you out of shit is your friend
3)and when you're in deep shit, keep your mouth shut.

CYNIC'S DICTIONARY OF TERMS

Chic: Considered smart without the deadening implication of intelligence.

Clique: A group of insiders who get outsiders with their backsides; a close circle of the asses.

Consultant: A jobless person who shows executives how to work.

Erudite: Exhibiting a degree of book learning fatal to success in any business or romantic enterprise.

Funeral home: A stately manse occupied by transients who continually receive visitors but lack the energy and inclination to entertain them.

Hip: smartly attuned to the latest cutting-edge clich=E9s.

Job: The state of employment everyone wants but if you look forward to on a Monday morning.

Lecher: A stud with liver spots.

Looting: a public shopping spree generously sponsored by local merchants in the wake of a riot.

Lottery: The equivalent of betting that the next pope will be from Duluth, or that the parrot in the pet store window speaks Flemish.

Mugger: A benevolent citizen of the streets who frequently spares the lives of total strangers in exchange for any cash and valuables in their possession.

Negotiating: The art of persuading your opponent to take the nice shiny copper penny and give you the wrinkled old paper money.

Revolutionary: An oppressed person waiting for the opportunity to become an oppressor.

Shallowness: The root cause of chronic good health, high school popularity, appearance on the fiction best-seller lists, and gainful employment on local TV news broadcasts.

Star: a performer who makes more than his or her agent.

Superstar: the performer who makes more than Guatemala.

State-of-the-art: Soon to be obsolete.

Taboo: Any strict cultural prohibition that, when breached, causes everyone in the group to gasp. e. g., Cannibalism, public nudity, serving fried pork rinds and a hedonistic wedding, or answering the question "how are you?" in the negative.

Unemployment: The usual alternative to overwork.

Virgin: A young innocent to in former times was sacrificed to the gods but now merely lives in disgrace.

Wake: 1) A convivial soiree with a preserved corpse in the room.

2) What the mourners would be visibly startled to see the corpse do, especially those expecting a sizable inheritance.